WOMAN
ALONE

WOMAN ALONE

Sailing Solo Across the Atlantic

Clare Francis

David McKay Company, Inc.
New York

Library of Congress Cataloging in Publication Data

Francis, Clare.
Woman alone.

   1. Observer Singlehanded Transatlantic Sailing Race.
2. Francis, Clare. I. Title.
GV832.F695 797.1′4   77-8708
ISBN 0-679-50758-2

10   9   8   7   5   4   3   2   1

MANUFACTURED IN THE UNITED STATES OF AMERICA

To J,
without whom neither would
have been finished

Acknowledgments

I would like to express my thanks to the following people and organizations. Ron and Joan Green for lending me their lovely boat; James Robertson and Sons for providing the finance; Margot Lovell for handling my publicity with such tact and diplomacy; Marconi (Coastal Radio Limited) for lending me one of their excellent Falcon II transmitters; Post Office Radio Station Portishead for being so helpful; my great ally, Jack Hill, for always being a delight to talk to; the *Daily Express;* Arthur Blackham and all at the Meteorological Office, Bracknell; the BBC World Service for broadcasting the forecasts; Chloride Automotive Batteries Limited for donating the battery-power; Joe Sanders of The Lymington Sail and Tent Company for providing hundreds of bits and pieces, as well as endless cups of coffee; Lucas Marine Limited for their excellent advice; Brookes and Gatehouse for their wonderful after-sales service; Camper and Nicholson Marine Equipment for finding charts on a Sunday morning; Henri-Lloyd and Onshore for the oilskins; Prewitt's, Jordan's, and the United Malting Co. for provisions.

I would also like to give my thanks to the Royal Western Yacht Club of England for organizing the race, to the *Observer* for sponsoring it, and to the U.S. Tobacco Company for providing the excellent liaison at the finish.

Finally, I would like to thank my family for their tremendous encouragement and support.

1

It was a very gray day like most of the days that autumn, although I could swear that North Devon was at least ten degrees grayer than anywhere else. The drizzle, which had been falling since September, was an uncompromising curtain of gloom, which exactly matched my mood. I sat in front of the typewriter and stared at the heading that had become only too familiar; "CHAPTER ONE" it read. The trouble was, it sat quite alone at the top of an empty page and had done so for about three weeks.

Having had no new thoughts for two hours, and no thoughts at all for the rest of the morning, I eased myself up from the desk and slipped down the road to see if there was any mail, knowing full well that I would continue to slip down the road until I came to the seashore, there to spend several hours being blown along the deserted beach wondering, among other things, how one became an instantly successful writer without being able to write one word. With a bit of luck and by the time I had done some shopping, Jacques should then be back from work and I could forget about that reproachful "CHAPTER ONE" until the next day.

I eyed my mail with some suspicion. Like many people who have their own boat, I couldn't really afford it. This means that my life was spent recovering from unexpected bills of such size that I had to steel myself when opening them.

This particular morning looked as though it would be no exception; there were two official-looking envelopes waiting for me, and rather than spoil my day so early, I pocketed them and set off for the beach. As I walked along the windswept sand, I reflected that my new career was not looking too bright. It was becoming increasingly clear to me that if I was a born writer, this fact was hiding itself extremely well. Regretfully it was time to think about finding something else to do.

Eighteen months before I had given up a job in marketing and sailed away alone to America and the West Indies, indulging a dream held since the day I had started sailing as a child of six. Originally I planned to travel with friends but then, on impulse, I spent the whole of Great Uncle Tom's legacy on a lovely 32 footer called *Gulliver G* and sailed the Atlantic singlehanded for a bet. On arrival I declared "never again" in a loud voice, and with two companions, traveled on to the Caribbean. By writing a few articles and taking Americans on day charters I managed to spend the whole of the next winter in the West Indies. But, beautiful though the islands were, I knew I didn't want to stay there. Nor did I want to cruise the world alone; I much preferred having friends aboard and, while they could manage a flight to the West Indies, I couldn't see many coming to join me in Tahiti.

But just as I was wondering what to do that next summer the perfect solution appeared. A girl named Trish found me, told me about an exciting two-handed race called the Round Britain, and within a few minutes we had agreed to become the first all-girl crew to take part. The only problem was money. Although we had a boat in *Gulliver G*, her sails were held together by sheer habit and my stitching, neither of which promised much in a bit of wind. But Trish had it all planned; she dashed back to England to find us a sponsor, and within an amazingly short time *Gulliver G* was faced with the ignominy of being renamed *Cherry Blossom* after a well-known English brand of shoe polish. I don't think she has ever forgiven me for it.

That I eventually did the Round Britain with Eve Bonham is a long story involving love, jet flights across the Atlantic, and a cast of thousands. It ended in Trish getting married just before the race. But Eve and I had a marvelous time and even managed to finish third on handicap, mainly because in anything upwards of a gale when most boats grind to a halt *Gulliver G* is just getting into her stride.

The Round Britain had been my introduction to long-distance racing, and I had loved it. It had also been my introduction to a breathtaking Frenchman with blond hair, a dark tan, and bright blue eyes. He was a world traveler by trade, working on or around boats to earn a passage. He had just returned from the Round the World Race in time to jump on a Round Britain boat as a substitute crew. He had no steady job, very little money, and I ran away with him in September.

Now in the fall of 1974 we were here in North Devon where Jacques had a job refitting a yacht. And here was I wondering what to do with my life. Of course there were other races to be sailed. There was the Azores and Back Singlehanded Race the next summer, and the following year, the classic Observer Singlehanded Transatlantic Race; events that were open to all kinds of boats and were not governed by the restrictive international racing regulations that required boats to be built "to the rules." Many friends from the Round Britain would be doing the Transatlantic Race and it was difficult not to get caught up in their enthusiasm. But as I kept reminding myself, I had no desire to sail singlehanded again. I had done it once and that was quite enough. Although, when I thought about it, racing would be very different.

3

There would be the excitement of the race not to mention the companionship of other competitors, unseen but very tangible. And there was the adventure, the greatest draw of all. But, I told myself sternly, the adventure will turn out to be no adventure of all, just the grim misery of being wet, cold, and miserable nearly all the time. It was ridiculous to even consider it; I really should settle down to looking after Jacques in a little "rose-covered cottage."

Yet, as I walked along the shore familiar thoughts kept nagging away at me; the same old chestnuts that I had fallen for before. Like "there's plenty of time for rose-covered cottages" and "you're only young once" and "won't it be a nice thing to remember when you're seventy." And more than anything there was the challenge. Just once more, said a little voice, just do the race and then run to seed with honor!

It was all very well, I said to myself, but what about all the other things a responsible person should consider. Such as my very loyal and long-suffering parents who, though extremely adaptable, had found the breathtaking rapid changes in my life a little difficult to adjust to. First I had given up my hard-won job with "grad, pension, comp. car, and fringe benefits" to sail off into the blue, then I had announced I was going singlehanded. It had been very hard for them to understand, and even more difficult for them to wait and worry during the 35 days of my passage to America. But afterward they had been very proud and had followed the Round Britain with great interest. However, more single-handing would subject them to more worry, and I was sure they would not like the idea. But, just to see if they would absolutely hate it, I had started chatting to them about the forthcoming races one day, not mentioning that I had so much as thought about entering them myself.

"Well," said Mother suddenly, "as long as you keep your safety harness clipped on. And, darling, *do* remember to eat well. That's the important thing!"

"No, no!" said Father emphatically. There was a long

pause while Mother and I waited expectantly. "The important thing's a good boat!"

If my parents had anticipated events, then Jacques had been miles ahead of them. "As soon as I've finished my job here we'll go to Lymington and start thinking about a boat for you," he happened to mention one day.

"But I haven't decided to go off and do the race yet," I pointed out.

He laughed. "After looking after me for a while, I won't be able to stop you!"

Suddenly we had begun making plans in earnest and what had just been an idea became a project. But we were immediately faced by two problems that seemed insurmountable. First there was the matter of a boat. I loved *Gulliver G* with all my heart. She was a fine sea boat and very tough with it but, even viewed from my biased view point, she was not fast. This would not matter so much in the Azores and Back Race. It was a shorter race for smaller boats, designed as a warm-up and qualifying race for the Transatlantic. But the big race itself was 3,000 miles long, from Plymouth to Newport, Rhode Island, and could take anything between three and a half and five weeks — or eight if you were feeling particularly relaxed about it. *Gulliver G* had done the crossing in five and a half weeks, but I would be very much happier to think I could be doing it in four. As the saying goes, it's not when you start talking to yourself that you should get worried, it's when you start replying. And I reckoned about four weeks was my replying time.

Also, I would be the first British woman to do the race and while I am no women's libber out to beat the men, at the same time I didn't want to let the side down. Based on the fantastic encouragement that hundreds of women had given Eve and me in the Round Britain, I knew that there would be a few women who would be very disappointed if I arrived toward the end of the Transatlantic fleet. And that might happen in *Gulliver G* if the winds were very much less than gale force. And if they were gale force I wouldn't be very happy anyway.

The biggest problem with *Gulliver G* was that she was distinctly overweight. She had a beautiful solid wood interior, but this added to her displacement and she was at least four inches down on her waterline. In theory I could strip her out, but I knew I could never bring myself to do it, for her lovely woodwork could never be replaced. Besides which, the cost would be enormous. And cost was the second problem.

If I raced *Gulliver G* just as she was, I could just manage to afford to race without buying any new sails or gear. But old and worn equipment has a habit of falling apart in mid-Atlantic and I wasn't too happy at that prospect. Ideally there should be a new boat, but since they started at five figures and went upward very quickly, there was not the vaguest chance of getting one.

The obvious solution was a sponsor, but not only had I chosen a bad economic year to want money, I had actually chosen the worst in twenty years. If I had asked almost any firm for £30,000, they would have turned deathly white and shown me the door. Even shoe polish was having a bad time. Cherry Blossom, who had shown enormous enthusiasm about more sponsorship, suddenly expressed the regret that they would be unable to help — their promotion budget had been cut in zero. But I wasn't entirely sorry about that; poor *Gulliver G* had been subjected to undignified taunts along the lines of, "Won't need antifouling with that stuff on the bottom," which were only surpassed by what Eve and I ourselves had to endure: "Which one's Cherry and which one's Blossom?"

So here I was without a suitable boat, without the finances to buy one, and if I was truthful, without much of a project at all. I was in the middle of one singularly unsuccessful attempt to graduate from being a sometime writer of yachting articles to a fully fledged author, and I didn't think I could face another change. The thought of staring at "CHAPTER

ONE" again — or as it often turned out when I started a new page, "CHPATER ONE" — filled me with dismay only surpassed by the thought of going back to work in an office.

Just to ensure there was no danger of being cheered up, when I returned to our house I opened the first of the two official-looking envelopes that had been in my mail that morning. It was a bill for what looked like "6 grummets, 5 sprockets, 1 patch to join others holding spinnaker together." The bill was from my sailmaker, Joe, at The Lymington Sail and Tent Company — a friend indeed. Most others would have refused to put another stitch in that spinnaker for fear of disturbing what remained of the material.

The second envelope contained a letter from a solicitor and I had to look at it three times before I believed what I saw. The letter read, "We have a Client on whose behalf we are inquiring whether you would be interested in sailing his and his wife's boat in the Azores and possibly the Transatlantic Race. The boat was constructed with singlehanding in view and is equipped with every electronic aid. . . ."

"Ah," said Jacques, looking over my shoulder. "How do you say it? A fairy godfather!"

We were quite sure that such things like winning the pools happened only to other people. We tried to temper our excitement with a little caution. Suppose the boat was completely unsuitable? Suppose there were unacceptable strings attached? Suppose it was a complete hoax. But if it was as good an offer as it sounded, it could be the most extraordinarily good luck in the world. I wrote back immediately and waited anxiously for a reply.

It came soon after. The people concerned were a Mr. and Mrs. R. Green of Croydon, and they would very much like me to come and have dinner, when they would tell me all about the boat, an Ohlson 38. Within two days I was in Croydon. I discovered that the offer was as good as it had sounded.

Ron and Joan Green's generosity was matched only by

their enthusiasm that I should sail their boat. They had built her specially for the Azores and Transatlantic races with the idea of lending her to a worthy entrant. How they decided on me I'm not too sure, but I think Joan had something to do with it, having followed Eve and me in the Round Britain. The boat was offered to me without conditions, excepting one: that I take her on a month's trial at the end of which I must decide whether I was happy with the boat. Now it was December and the weather was freezing, but with no time to lose Jacques and I gritted our chattering teeth, gloved our blue and frozen hands, and sailed out of Chichester whenever we could to test the vessel.

After a few weekends it was clear that the Ohlson went like a rocket in everything but very light airs. She was sleek, long, and elegant, and carried a weight of sail. But our first worry was that she might be altogether too much for me. She was a much larger boat than I was used to and almost certainly more than I could handle comfortably. Her genoas were twice the size of *Gulliver G's* and a lot more effort was required to hoist them up and sheet them in.

Another problem was that the boat tended to heel easily. This meant that she had to have exactly the right amount of sail up when on or close to the wind. Too much and she was over on her ear, too little and there was no longer the power to push her through the seas. This meant a lot of sail changes, something the singlehanders would rather avoid as they are the most tiring part of the job.

Jacques was particularly worried about this as he watched me trying to pull a large sail on deck. I wobbled dangerously over the forehatch, puffing and panting with the effort. "I'm just unfit," I wheezed, which was true.

"Huhh," grunted Jacques, "more like you're just not big enough."

But despite these problems we both knew the opportunity was too good to miss and that it would be madness not to accept a boat with such potential. Ron and Joan were delighted to hear the news and as always were very generous in their offers of assistance and support. Ron even insisted on paying for some new gear for the boat, something for which I was very grateful, because in a short month we had managed to draw up a very long list of things that needed to be done, most of which would be very expensive. It was clear that, despite Ron's help, the usual financial gap was going to yawn in front of us. But at least the gap was very much smaller than the price of a new boat. Full of hope, I started the long search for the only answer to the problem: a commercial sponsor.

I am quite sure that many companies have a file marked "Crazies" and that my request for sponsorship went into it. It's a feeling one got from their replies, which had the patient tone a parent adopts when explaining to a child that unfortunately there were no sweets to be had today. Perhaps I shouldn't have sent a photo; people expect a singlehanded sailing lady to sport enormous biceps, baggy jeans, and a jolly manner. Being a bit sensitive about this image, I had sent a particularly glamorous (for me) picture that would suggest, I hoped, that the newsmen would surround me in droves, creating lots of publicity for my generous sponsor. Instead, at least one company said they couldn't believe that a little thing like me could possibly manage to cross the Atlantic alone, and they would not like to encourage me to do so.

Fifty letters later I was feeling a bit despondent. Some companies had even returned my letter unopened, which I became incensed about, saying what was the country coming to and were we living in a police state or what? Then Jacques pointed out that, if I cared to look on the envelopes, I might see that I had forgotten to put any stamps on them.

The year before, when looking for sponsorship for the Round Britain, I had written to my old employers, Robertson's (the jam and marmalade firm). They had replied that they had no money to spare, and when was I going to stop loafing around the Caribbean making them mad with envy? I had long since given them up as a possible sponsor, but happened to phone Mike Leach, my ex-colleague and

9

now marketing director to have a chat. Mike, who had the habit of leaning back in his chair at a dangerous angle, promptly fell off it on hearing my voice, doubtless at the memory of my filing system. But, after the dreadful clatter at the other end of the telephone had subsided, we exchanged news.

"And so you're going on with this racing?" asked Mike.

"Yes, but I've got to find some firm with pots of money and no idea of how to spend it," I replied disconsolately. "There must be a gullible marketing director around with more money than brains, but I'm having a hard job finding him."

"Oh, I don't know," replied Mike, "write me a letter and we'll see."

Which is how the Ohlson 38 came to be called *Robertson's Golly*, complete with a painting of the firm's symbol, a golliwog on each bow.

When asking for money for a boat, one must bear in mind that one stainless-steel bolt can cost five pounds and a radio transmitter four thousand. I added up the cost of everything I thought I needed, tried to pretend it didn't look enormous, and handed it to Robertson's. They were able to let me have a tenth of the figure. But I was not complaining; all help was gratefully received. And now we could at least get some of the essential jobs done by buying sensibly and doing all the work ourselves.

By the New Year we had moved onto *Gulliver G* at Lymington and, with the *Golly* berthed next door, were able to start work in earnest. While I tried to earn some money by writing articles and struggling on with the book, doomed never to be published, Jacques did most of the donkey work. We changed the rig back from a cutter to a sloop as she was originally designed to be. The foredeck had been too cluttered with the extra inner forestay. The running backstays, necessary to support it, were an added complication. I preferred a simple rig that had no weaknesses, for my one dread was of something going seriously wrong in the middle of nowhere. With this in mind, we also removed the grooved forestay, which was designed to make sail changing easier. It had already gone wrong once, jamming a sail in its track. There was no way I could remedy such a fault when alone at sea. A sail jammed up the track would mean the end of the race and a long hazardous trip back to harbor. We therefore changed to a normal wire forestay and had good old-fashioned hanks put on the sails. It would be more work for me to change sail, but at least I would have one less thing to worry about.

Another major task we thought essential was to change the existing self-steering gear for a Gunning. The existing gear was the old-fashioned vertically pivoted vane type, marvelous for well-balanced, undercanvased cruising boats, but not for the *Golly* at full speed; it didn't begin to control her. Gunning gear is the most powerful and yet sensitive gear I have ever come across. *Gulliver G* had been fitted with one and I had had a lot of experience with it. Not that it is the most elegant piece of gear in the world. In fact, it closely resembled a piece of agricultural machinery and the uninitiated might suspect that Rube Goldberg had had a wild and unrestricted hand in its design. Many were the times I found a small crowd gathered around the stern staring in awe at the gear's many arms, ropes, and protuberances, wondering, no doubt, how many bales of hay it made to the acre.

There were hundreds of other jobs to do, most small, but all time-consuming. All spare moments were spent sailing, trying to tune the boat and get the best out of her. But time is always too short when preparing a boat and soon June and *Yachting Monthly's* Azores and Back Singlehanded Race were only weeks away.

I was a little worried about the lack of sea miles I had done in the *Golly,* having sailed only the minimum 300 miles singlehanded to qualify for the race, and another 500 miles with Jacques. I would have liked to find out how the boat weathered a gale before starting out into the Atlantic, but a convenient gale never came along, which was inevitable when we were mad enough to want one.

As it happened, it couldn't have mattered less; the Azores Race was remarkable for the steady following wind on the way down and the almost total lack of wind on the way back. The worst moment for me was arriving in the Azores with the prospect of spending ten days there without Jacques. Before the race we had decided the air fare was far too expensive, but after a couple of days in port I decided it would have been cheap at double the price and telegraphed a desperate message to England. Luckily I didn't have long to wait; Jacques had already booked on the next plane out.

I finished tenth out of more than 50 boats in the Azores Race, a result I was very pleased with. The light winds had not been ideal for the *Golly;* she was not light enough to bounce over the big ocean swell without wind and was easily overtaken by the very light displacement boats in these conditions. So a tenth place was no disappointment. And I knew that, in the very mixed conditions of the North Atlantic, she would come into her own.

The Azores Race had been conceived as a warm-up and qualifying race for people who wanted to enter the Transatlantic Race in the Jester Class (for boats under 38 feet in length). But on arrival back in Falmouth there was a bad outbreak of "Never Again" sickness, and it looked as though few people would be going on to do the longer race. "Never Again" disease affects most sailing people at some time in their careers and is particularly virulent after a gale or a long ocean passage. It affects singlehanders nearly all the time, and the yacht club bar at Falmouth rang with such confident statements as "Well, I've done a long passage singlehanded now, and once is quite enough. Never again!" Those with several long singlehanded passages behind them nodded sagely, winked among themselves, and smiled in a knowing way, much to the irritation of the Never Again-ers, who restated their feelings with some emphasis.

Later not only did many of the Never Again-ers enter the Transatlantic Race, but also most of them denied ever having the intention of doing otherwise!

12

Encouraged by my placing in the AZAB, I was not one of the "Never Again" types. I entered, later that summer, in the L'Aurore Race for singlehanders. Competing in level-racing boats supplied by the sponsor, the event is particularly tough because it requires the participants to cross the Channel several times. It is an affair noteworthy for the amount of sleep one misses because of the hazards of shoals, tides and currents, and coastwise shipping. I placed fifth out of 12 entrants in the race — all top-notch French sailors — which was particularly satisfying.

With the coming of the autumn of 1975 I had to make the final decision whether to go ahead with my plans for the Transatlantic Race. It would need another winter of preparation and a spring of sailing to be ready for the start on June 5, 1976. At this stage I had to be sure I wanted to do the race, for once committed, it is always difficult to pull out and disappoint those who have put a lot of work into the project.

The Observer Singlehanded Transatlantic Race (OSTAR for short) is not a race to be undertaken lightly. The shortest route between Plymouth and Newport, Rhode Island, is 2,800 miles long and takes you through shipping, icebergs, and thick fog. It also exposes you to the North Atlantic weather, which is unpredictable at best. Although one may be sure that it will be very stormy and unpleasant in winter, the inverse is rarely true in summer. One may expect at least one gale, but probably more, and storms or hurricanes are not unknown even in the very middle of summer.

The prevailing North Atlantic winds are westerly, so that, in racing from east to west, one is constantly battling to windward. Of course this is what makes the race difficult and, I kept reminding myself, very uncomfortable, undoubtedly wet, and certainly miserable. There were more pleasant routes to choose from. One could go south on the Azores route as I had done in 1973. It was longer, at 3,500 miles, but much sunnier and less prone to strong winds. Or, if one really wanted a nice time, one went far south to the trade winds, which blew steadily from behind. But at 4,200 miles this route was so long one was in danger of missing all the parties in Newport at the end of the race, quite apart from running out of books to read on route.

But if I was to do the race, I was determined to take the direct route, also known as the Great Circle or northern route. On this route a conventional, single-hulled boat could capitalize on her best asset: her ability to go to windward, while the multihulled catamarans and trimarans would search for beam winds farther south. Ever since the first race in 1960, the winning boats had taken a more or less direct route, and I was certain the *Golly* was best suited to the conditions that were found there; that is, medium to strong headwinds.

There were other routes, like the Far North Route, which was easily discounted as the very sound of it made me shiver. And there was the Rhumb Line or constant-compass course. But no other route appealed to me like the Northern Route for the simple reason that, if I was to race at all, I wanted to take what promised to be the quickest way to Newport.

Gales, fogs, icebergs — it was not a very pleasant outlook viewed from almost any angle and, when I thought about it too much, I decided that perhaps I might quietly change my mind about the race and go cruising instead. But in the end I always managed to overlook all the reasons *not* to do the race and would find myself making plans again, as if I had never had a moment's doubt. And, when I thought about them, the reasons *in favor* of doing the race were as attractive as ever. There is never a clear-cut reply to that eternal question "Why?" And I can symphathize wholeheartedly with the ladies of the town if, as one is led to believe, they are constantly being asked the same question as I am: "What makes a nice girl like you do what you do?" A short answer such as "Because I like it," merely mystifies the questioner more.

But for me the main attraction was undoubtedly the race itself. Variously described by the newspapers as "the toughest race in the world," "the last great struggle between one man and the sea'' which was laying it on a bit thick, and "an impossible race in improbable craft," which may have been nearer the point, the race was none of these things to me. It was, simply, a great adventure in which you had to pit your wits and your skill against the sea.

To go singlehanded was to add to the satisfaction and feeling of achievement — once you had arrived. During the race itself, being alone would be a hardship that had to be endured, rather than a luxury to be enjoyed. Contrary to belief, singlehanders are not always loners. In fact, many of them hate being alone under normal circumstances (that includes me) and are often the most gregarious of people who can be relied upon to be the life and soul of any party.

Many friends from the Round Britain would be taking part, and a motley crew they were too. The parties before the race, and doubtless the reminiscences after, promised great things. And during the race there would be a perverse kind of pleasure in knowing that one's mates were getting blown at, rained on, battered about and were generally wet, cold, and miserable too.

There were risks of course — from collision with a ship, an iceberg, or some large jetsam, from illness or accident, from falling overboard, or from excessively bad weather. But many sports involve risk, and certainly an adventure is no adventure without it. And it is that element of uncertainty that provides the extra something — fright when at sea, but a lovely feeling of relief on arrival.

I had now to decide whether the loneliness, the sheer discomfort, and the likelihood of being frightened a great deal of the time were going to be worth that nice feeling of achievement I hoped to enjoy after the finish. Looked at from a rational point of view I should probably have stayed at home, but somehow I always knew I wouldn't.

Besides which, this was going to be my last big race before carrying out my firm intention of running to fat in a "rose-covered cottage." And how could I say "Never again" with any conviction if I hadn't had a really horrible time?

15

2

To sail the Atlantic singlehanded takes a great deal of physical effort and one should, ideally, be very fit indeed.

"Must get fit," I announced after a particularly greedy Christmas. "Running at dawn, visits to the gym, sensible food, no alcohol . . . ."

"Great! I'll sit back and watch," said Jacques with the self-satisfied air of the working man. Tired of the vagaries of the boat fitting and delivery businesses, he had taken a job as a French teacher in Basingstoke for which, everyone was surprised to discover, he was fully qualified.

"Why don't you start properly and run around the valley at six tomorrow morning?" he smiled innocently. We had taken a rented farmhouse in Berkshire, the nearest place we could find to Jacques's new job. The lovely house had an unspoiled view of the Pang Valley, which was perfect running country with its many quiet country lanes.

"Splendid idea," I exclaimed. "Up at six and a quiet two-mile trot to start with. Don't want to overdo it."

At eight the next morning I jumped guiltily out of bed and

17

trotted off into the mist thinking lots of healthy thoughts about clean, natural living and good exercise. Ten minutes later I lay flat on my back on the sofa, clutching my pounding head and wondering if my heart was up to the job.

Jacques viewed my panting form with interest. "That was quick," he remarked unnecessarily. "Perhaps you should have been a sprinter."

And that was the end of my special training, except for a few quick darts around the marina when I was feeling especially overfed or unprepared. "The sailing'll get me fit," I kept saying in a confident voice, hoping desperately it would, for I only had to think of winching in the *Golly's* headsails to make me feel decidedly nervous.

We started work again on the boat in February and there was no danger of getting any exercise out of it; I spent most of my time motionless, frozen by the cold. But the boat's bottom had to be painted and, with the aid of Ron and his helpers, we splashed on the antifouling as best we could, our arms stiff and our hands chilled. Luckily Ron had had the foresight to provide a flask of something fiery to thaw the stomach, and the working party frequently retired to the cabin for refreshments. It took a long time to get the boat painted but everyone enjoyed it immensely.

There were many other jobs to be done before the *Golly* would be ready for the new season. Ron kindly furnished more cabin windows to provide more light for the inside of the boat, only two ports having originally been fitted so as not to reduce the strength of the coach roof. But we all felt the boat was quite strong enough to take more windows and fitted the remainder without a qualm. And what a difference it made to the interior. It cheered me up enormously; the North Atlantic would be gray enough without trying to block out the light. A new forehatch was also fitted for the good reason that the old fiberglass hatch leaked like a sieve. Fiberglass hatches are almost impossible to make watertight. We had spent hours edging the rims with rubber gaskets but, the hatch being infinitely

18

flexible, it would become watertight at one point, only to let in water at another. But the new Canpa hatch was a great improvement. Not only did it never let in a drop of water — and the *Golly* was a wet boat to windward — but I could open it from on deck, essential for a singlehander. It is frustrating to be on the foredeck and be unable to reach a sail except by trotting back along the deck to the main hatch, through the cabin, and into the sail locker to open the hatch from below. And you may be sure that, at the precise moment you open the hatch and stick your head out, some water will slip across the deck and hit you dead in the eye.

Another improvement was a folding propeller. This was part of Ron's go-fast strategy. "Should give you an extra quarter knot," he announced proudly, "another five percent on your average speed. Bring you in ten days ahead of everyone else." Ron's optimism was boundless. One day I went down to the boat to find a black stripe had been painted along the hull just above the waterline. "Makes you go faster," said Ron, refusing to be drawn further, although he did wink in the direction of another competitor's boat and tap the side of his head several times, which I took to indicate that there was some psychological warfare going on.

In his desire to provide me with the fastest boat in the world Ron also became convinced that the *Golly* was too heavy. "All those teak fittings could come out, you know," he would say. "Could strip her out completely in a day." I thought of the stripped-out boats I had seen with canvas bunks, a bucket for a head, and a single gas ring on which to cook. Then I looked at the *Golly* with her teak-faced woodwork, comfortable bunks, and soft cushions to sleep on; her well-fitted galley with its gimbaled stove with two burners, grill, and oven; her proper fixed head which could not be knocked over. There was no doubt in my mind. Life was too short and racing not important enough to take things to extremes; the trip would be uncomfortable enough without actually trying to make it miserable.

With comfort in mind, I had also got my heart set on a cabin heater. Many people had warned me about the cold temperatures near the Grand Banks of Newfoundland where the wind can blow straight off the ice and freeze you to the bone. It was a depressing picture, but made far less so by the vision of a cozy little cabin with a glowing heater by which to warm my hands. We chose a Taylor's kerosene heater because it produced a moistureless heat — very important for drying out a damp cabin — and because it used a fuel I understood, another important consideration. As usual Jacques was the only one with the expertise to fit it, and it joined the pile of jobs awaiting his attention on the weekends. I hated to see him working every weekend after a hard week at school and often suggested getting the yard to do some of the work. "What, and pay their prices!" he would retort, hammering another bit of wood into place. "Not until I drop."

However some jobs had to be done in the yard and the bill was indeed large. Robertson's had kindly come up with more sponsorship for the year but my outgoings were rapidly expanding to absorb it. Quite apart from the yard bill, there was much more expensive gear to be bought and many additional costs to be met, such as my air fare back from America. Robertson's, who were the most undemanding sponsors ever, had asked only that I return to England as soon as possible after the race, so that I could do some publicity work for them. And this suited me very well — one Atlantic sea crossing per year was quite enough. However, this left the problem of how to get the boat back from America — yet another item to add to my list of Things to Remember.

Although I could afford to buy some much-needed equipment that year, there was no way the money would stretch to a radio-telephone and this was the one thing that I desperately wanted. I was sure it would make all the difference to my morale. It is one thing to be alone and another to feel totally isolated; if I could talk to my family and Jacques I would never feel too depressed or lonely.

I suspected that the major manufacturers of long-range transmitters must get hundreds of requests from poverty-stricken sailors in search of a set on loan, so I knew I was very lucky when Marconi agreed to lend me one. The set was a Falcon II, capable of transmitting up to 400 miles on medium frequency, and 3,000 on high frequency. It was a marvelous piece of equipment, but it required power and a lot of it. This posed a whole new set of problems, few of which I understood. Fortunately I went to Lucas for advice and, having it all explained to me several times and in language I could understand, I had a clear picture of what was needed. Basically I had to be able to run the main engine generator while transmitting if I was to get sufficient power. This meant additional alternators, screened control boxes, and extra batteries, kindly donated by Chloride. By the end of the exercise the technical terms fell from my lips as from an electronic engineer's.

Marconi took infinite pains over the fitting and tuning of the radio, testing each preset frequency time and time again while I hovered around the set, watching anxiously. Although I had exuded confidence in my letters to Marconi, the truth was that I had only a smattering of knowledge about radios. I knew how to tune into Radio 2 and how to find a Coastal Radio Beacon, but that was child's play compared to this.

"Easy," said Jacques, you just pick up the telephone thing and speak." I had the feeling he was oversimplifying matters but as it turned out there really wasn't much more to it than that, in theory at least. To make a call I had to contact the Post Office Radio station at Portishead near Bristol and they would then link me into the telephone network. To get an idea of how the system worked I went down to the station to meet the operators and listen in on some calls. They were immensely helpful and very interested to meet a person who would normally be just a voice

21

to them. "Don't worry," they said, "we'll listen for you through all the other traffic. Although you'll be pretty weak, of course."

"I will?" I asked anxiously.

"Only compared to the big ships," they said. "But don't worry, we'll hear you."

I hoped they were right. Thinking it might serve as a small reminder, I sent them a couple of photographs of me and the boat with my radio call sign in large letters at the top and the postscript "Listen for the quiet small voice in the night — it might be me shouting!"

Gradually I got to know the radio and, with the help of Marconi, I even learned how to replace fuses and make other minor repairs. "But one thing," they warned me, *"whatever you do, don't let the radio get wet!"* "Of course not," I promised, knowing full well that even the nicest boats seem dry in harbor, but quickly turn into garden sprinklers given sufficient pressure of water on the deck. But as always Mother came to the rescue and, with measurements and waterproof material in hand, disappeared in the direction of her sewing machine to emerge two hours later with a cover that was destined to repel many gallons of water from the direction of my precious radio.

The work on the boat seemed endless and the number of jobs ever multiplying. Of all my lists the one headed Things to Do was always by far the longest, for no sooner had one item been crossed off the top than another would be added at the bottom. Modern yachts must be the most complex pieces of sporting equipment yet thought of; if it were just a matter of tuning up the rigging and getting a reasonably good set to the sails the matter would be considerably more simple. But there were so many other things to be fitted, maintained, or repaired: electrics, engines, and generators; pumps, spare pumps, and emergency pumps; radios and navigation instruments with their dials and repeaters; the compass and spare compass.

Spares had to be found for everything and I had to learn how to fit them, which was sometimes easy but more often difficult, as in the case of the main engine. In a sailing race an engine is not usually important, but I was going to use the Volvo Penta to generate power for all the electrics on board as well as the transmitter. Although diesels are very reliable, they can get air or dirt in their tubes, problems that are simple to fix if you know how. But I was never sure I did, and I could only hope that I would never have to put my wobbly expertise to the test.

Without Jacques's help the boat would never have been ready. Every weekend he brought his marvelously practical eye to bear on the most impossible of problems, finding solutions so simple and straightforward that I was always filled with admiration. He would ponder problems while sucking on a pipe, his thoughtful face hidden in wreaths of smoke, and then, as an idea formed, he would give a contented grunt and amble into action. Once I was horrified to see smoke emerging from a cockpit locker and, grabbing a fire extinguisher I rushed to douse the flames only to discover that Jacques was lying in the bottom of the locker, his pipe firmly locked between his teeth, planning the route of a new sink outlet.

There was very little that Jacques's skill could not fix; he was a good carpenter, a first-rate fitter, and a marvelous shipwright. And yet there was one problem that he could not solve and this was the matter of the notorious toerail. The *Golly* had a smart-looking metal toerail to match her black metal mast. It was fixed onto the joint of the hull and deck by metal bolts every two inches. Each one of these bolts, and there were hundreds of them, let in water. It might have been possible to take out each bolt, fill the hole with sealant, and replace the bolt, but many of the nuts had been glassed in from underneath or hidden by interior fittings and, short of tearing out the interior and taking off the entire rail to start again — a mammoth job — there was no solution. Instead we decided to tackle the worst spots over the chart table and leave the rest. This meant that every locker had to be specially lined to keep the contents away from the sides of the hull where the water ran down. Most of the leaks produced only tiny amounts of water, but it takes only a little moisture to make clothes damp or food moldy.

"That toerail," or "that wetrail" as it was more often called, was a continuous source of annoyance to Jacques because he couldn't fix it, and to me because I always live under the optimistic illusion that my next voyage is going to be a dry and comfortable one.

Once the boat was back in the water, we also had to find time to go sailing. We wanted to try out a new device for furling the spinnaker, a kind of sock that slid down over it, and to find an easier way for me to handle the big foresails. While the spinnaker sock worked well, the problem of jib handling seemed insuperable. Although the boat was fitted with large winches some of which had three different speeds, even Jacques found the sails difficult to raise and sheet in. But, on the principle that one can do anything if one tries hard enough, I concluded that everything would take me a long time and a lot of effort, but I would always manage it in the end. Thus, while the musclemen racing sailors at Cowes Week may attack a winch with gorillalike ferocity and have a sail winched up in seconds, the same maneuver would take me five minutes with rests in between.

"Method is the important thing," I announced to Jacques one day. "If I put my foot here, and lean this way, I'll use only half the energy." I started to winch in the large genoa, puffing and panting with the effort. "There, nearly in," I wheezed, my face turning purple. The next moment I was sprawled over the winch, my chin resting on a life line, with the genoa flapping wildly in the breeze.

"Right, no more method!" said Jacques angrily. "Far too dangerous. I'd rather your biceps looked like a wrestler's."

"That's what you say now!" I wheezed and asked him how he'd like my biceps at fifty when they were large and flabby.

But he had a point. Everything on the *Golly* was so large and powerful that safety was the most important consideration. Without care, it was too easy to be swiped by a spinnaker pole or, dreadful to contemplate, be knocked overboard and see the boat sail away without you. But it was not always easy to avoid some tricky moments. Once, when lifting a heavy sail up from the deck to push it down the forehatch, I lost my balance and followed the sail down into the sailbin head first.

But these problems apart, I felt that the boat and I were going well together, and with each sail in the Solent or along the coast, I became more confident about the forthcoming race.

What a race it was to be. An incredible number of boats had entered the event — nearly 200, compared to five in the first race and what was considered to be the enormous number of 55 in the 1972 race. Sadly though, the press was full of criticism of the forthcoming event. Not that it had ever received the approval of the establishment who considered it "unseamanlike and irresponsible" because the singlehander could not keep a good lookout. And this time they had real fuel for their ammunition. Not only were there a large number of entries but the size of one boat was so vast that it was capable of sinking a ship. Alain Colas's *Club Méditerranée* was 236 feet long, more than six times the length of the *Golly!*

There was no size limit in the race because it was never believed that one person could handle a boat more than 50 feet long. But the size had crept up and now everyone was dismayed to see this monster appear, for it was capable of sinking some innocent vessel unconnected with the race. This altered the whole character of the event, the principle being that the only life at risk was your own. I think it was true to say that, with the best will in the world, most competitors wished *Club Med* a nasty mishap before the start.

But monsters apart, the race was promising to be anything but dull with 27 different nationalities entered in a variety of craft that embraced almost every shape and size of boat that could be propelled by sail. I was glad to hear that an Italian and two French girls had entered because, much as one gets fussed over when the only girl in the fleet, it is a little overwhelming to be outnumbered by 200 to 1. Another Italian girl had hoped to enter but had withdrawn after becoming pregnant. As someone pointed out, this was very wise because, even if she had started the race, she would have been disqualified for arriving in Newport with a crew.

As the race drew nearer, so the interest in it grew and the press began to turn up at Lymington in increasing numbers to interview the only British female competitor. Of course this was what sponsorship was all about and, sporting Robertson's emblem on my sweaters, I posed for endless numbers of "smilies" as Jacques called them, with either a coil of rope in hand (by far the favorite prop), a life belt over the shoulder, or a sail being stitched (not a typical pose). While these pictures were being taken Jacques would skulk below muttering darkly about "ridiculous poses" and "you won't be smiling like that in the middle of the Atlantic." But I had given up trying to change photographers' ideas years before. It was no good just being yourself, sitting there on the side of the boat. If you were a girl then you had to be smiling, and if you went sailing you had to be shown doing something nautical.

Not that I didn't get a lot of fun out of it, for many photographers would back tantalizingly close to the edge of the dock and keep me in fine suspense while they hovered near the water. And then there was the photographer who, in his efforts to get an unusual shot, suspended himself over the water and had his ear nibbled by Fred, our pet swan in search of his daily ration of bread. But the most spectacular of all was the BBC technician who, in his keenness to help tie the boat up, leaped straight off the *Golly's* bows into the sea. Apart from an initial shriek as he hit the ice-cold water he was really very good about it and, once he was able to breathe again, managed a very sporting imitation of a laugh.

Most photographers were happy with the inevitable coil of rope, but on one occasion I allowed myself to be pressured into wearing a bikini. I was unhappy about it — after all they don't ask the men sailors to pose in bathing trunks — but the photographer was obstinate and I thought it easier to give in and get it over with quickly. As I posed shivering beside the mast I suddenly noticed the photographer looking nervously behind him. "Do you have a dog aboard?" he asked. Not as far as I knew, I replied. "Then what's that growling?" he demanded.

The growling noise got louder and soon emerged from the main hatch in the form of Jacques, his teeth bared in a menacing snarl. I stepped hastily between him and the photographer. "What," he asked threateningly, "has this photograph to do with sailing the Atlantic?"

"Now, darling," I began soothingly.

"Does this twit really imagine you dress like that to pull up the mainsail?"

"Well, no . . ."

"What does he think this is . . . Playboy!"

The photographer retreated steadily down the deck, looking anxiously for an escape route. Jacques, his English exhausted, strode after him breathing torrents of what was undoubtedly very rude French.

It was the last time I posed in a bikini on the boat, though I did pose in one at the farm for the simple reason that it happened to be what I was wearing to weed the spinach patch when a photographer unexpectedly arrived. But, though I attempted to hide the newspaper in which the picture appeared, my family and friends waved it around with screams of delight and voted it photograph of the year. It showed me standing in the middle of the vegetable patch and was captioned "Clare Trains on Spinach," which prompted innumerable renderings of "Popeye the Sailorman" and as many pointed looks at the size of my biceps.

But if the gentlemen of the press were sometimes a little unfeeling, Jack Hill more than made up for them. For the duration of the race I had agreed to send reports to the *Daily Express* three times a week by radio, and Jack Hill, who was their southern area reporter, was to be my contact. Not only was Jack a sailing man who lived in Lymington, but also a tremendously kind and understanding person for whom nothing was too much trouble. It was he who was to dash across Lymington in the middle of the night and save me from abandoning the race, and he who was to cheer me through many a bleak moment in the weeks to come.

In addition to reporting for the *Express,* I was asked by the BBC to take a sound camera for their "The World About Us" series. I was anxious not to take on anything that was too difficult or time-consuming and, my expertise with cameras being limited to a simple still camera and home movies, I could see that a sound camera would fall into both the very difficult and very time-consuming categories.

"But it'll be dead simple!" said Bob Saunders, the director. "A small camera with built-in automatic sound, and all you'll have to do is press the switch and speak into the microphone. Really nothing to it!" If Bob hadn't been completely sincere I would have strangled him on arrival at Newport.

The Easter holidays gave Jacques and me the opportunity to take the *Golly* on a final tryout cruise across the Channel to Cherbourg, the Channel Islands, and St. Malo. For the first leg of the trip we joined a Chichester Yacht Club rally led and organized by Ron in his own boat, *Touchwood Too*. The rally, a thinly disguised excuse for having a marvelous time in France, was a great success. But the rest of our cruise was to be less than happy. Five hours out of Cherbourg en route for Guernsey I called up another yacht on the radio, heard an ominous hum from the set's power unit, and the next moment it went dead. Despite changing all the fuses and the main tube we were quite unable to make the radio work again. I was very depressed about it. If it happened during the race, not only would I be unable to contact anyone, but my family would imagine the worst. This was a powerful argument against having a radio and I could now appreciate how helpless I would feel if it broke down miles from anywhere.

After visiting St. Malo we became gale-bound in Guernsey, finally nosing our way out when we thought the wind had moderated. But it was only a temporary lull and we soon found ourselves struggling against a strong northerly. The wind showed no sign of change so there was no point in returning to Guernsey and hoping for it to moderate. We decided to carry on toward the Alderney Race, although the prospect of trying to sail through that unpleasant stretch of water was daunting, to say the least. If we tried to get through with both the tide and wind against us we would, quite simply, never make it. Indeed, in that strong current we would go very firmly backward. We must arrive at the Race with a fair tide, although this would mean struggling through steep breaking seas caused by the strong wind blowing against the current.

To be sure of catching the fair tide we pushed the *Golly* harder and harder into the wind, and she loved it, throwing up spray as she beat into the rising wind and waves. But we were not so happy. We became increasingly damp and miserable as more and more water came over the deck and seeped below. Worse, there appeared to be a lot of water finding its way into the boat from elsewhere. Every time I pumped the bilge it seemed to be full again in no time, slopping up into lockers and running over the floorboards. Investigation soon revealed the source of the trouble. The cockpit seats were not draining properly and the water that was accumulating on them was running down into the boat.

For a while I thought we would get through the Race without encountering large seas, but suddenly they were there in front of us. Very steep waves that were the most difficult for a small boat to get through. In a way I was glad we had found them. If the *Golly* could fight her way through these, then she could cope with almost anything. And fight she did, corkscrewing this way and that, digging her nose into a wave and rising suddenly to throw it off. Twice she lurched badly, falling sideways with a suddenness that frightened us, but in reponse to the helm she soon recovered and headed into the walls of water again. Once she leaped off a wave and found nothing but air on the other side, falling with a terrible crash into the water below. For a moment we thought something important like the mast or the hull must have broken, but we were relieved to find nothing worse than the compass turned inside out and the small rotating log pushed up into its housing in the hull.

Once clear of the Race I didn't have to ask Jacques how he felt about altering course for Cherbourg. One look at his miserable face and I knew he was as wet, cold, and tired as I was. And, though he was bravely trying to conceal it, he was feeling more than a little sick too.

But our heavy weather trial wasn't over yet. After a dry-out in Cherbourg we set off across the Channel to Lymington and, yet again, it blew hard from the north. Soon the boat was running with water and we were back to pumping every five minutes. Leaving the boat on self-steering, one of us rested while the other pumped. Then, as we neared England, I heard a nasty crack and was horrified to see that the tiller had split in two.

"Oh no!" I groaned as we lashed the tiller together, "what next?"

Next, it was the self-steering itself. The whole of the

lower section of the gear was designed to swing from side to side like a pendulum, pulling on the tiller lines to steer the boat, but it had to be prevented from swinging too far and hitting the main support section. The manufacturer recommended fitting preventer lines for this, an eminently creative Rube Goldberg solution, and I was not surprised to find that the strains of the long hard passage had proved too great and the lines had broken.

"Thank God it all happened *now*," gasped Jacques, "think how terrible it would have been to discover all this in the middle of the Atlantic."

"Please," I said, very quietly indeed, "don't even mention it."

A wet leaky boat, a tiller that came away in your hand, a radio that wasn't working, and a steering gear that was trying to do itself in, not the best of news just weeks before the race.

3

Luckily, everything seemed brighter the next day and, after listing what had to be done, we cheerfully set to work. Jacques rebedded every single deck fitting, while I lined the cockpit lockers with rubber strips that promised to be more watertight. We found that the tiller had been fitted with bolts that were far too small and it was these that had sheared, so we fitted much larger ones. Jacques also made a spare tiller just in case something similar should happen again.

The ever-patient Marconi man appeared and investigated the truant radio. He soon established that, much to my relief, the breakdown was not my fault, nor indeed any fault in the set itself. It was the wildly fluctuating power supply peculiar to a yacht that had confused the power unit and caused it to overheat. The power unit was soon modified and from that day on the radio was as reliable as an old workhorse.

The self-steering problem was not so easy to overcome. I fitted heavier preventer lines to replace the broken ones, but I was unhappy that they should be necessary at all. I felt the gear should be designed to swing freely from side to side without having to be prevented from hitting its main support, but no modification seemed possible and the company that made the gear could offer no suggestions. Apart from this, the gear did work superbly well and, pushing the doubts into the back of my mind, I laid in a good stock of spare preventer lines and forgot about it. It was to be a sad mistake.

Once these improvements and repairs had been carried out Jacques and I felt the *Golly* was ready for the race. The bad weather had been a blessing in disguise, not only for revealing weaknesses that we had been able to put right before the start, but also for showing us how well the *Golly* behaved in bad conditions. I felt confident that she could weather almost anything the Atlantic could produce, including hurricanes, although I hoped she would not be put to the test.

The last two weeks before the race were hectic, with more to be done than ever. With my list of provisions in hand I went off to the local supermarket and returned groaning with heavy boxes of food. Although I am a small eater, I find it very difficult not to set off on a voyage without enough food to feed six people for a month, or me alone for ten months. I decide on what to take by listing all the foods I like, estimating how much I'll eat in a week, and then multiplying that amount by the number of weeks I expect to be at sea — plus a bit more for greed.

This time I hoped to do the crossing in four weeks. For instance, in working out how much cheese to take, I reckoned one pound a week, which equaled four pounds of cheese, with a bit to spare, say five pounds in all. This system would have worked wonderfully except that my imagination is always larger than my stomach. I like many varieties of tinned fruit, but instead of taking a few of each, I applied my standard calculation to each variety. In this way the lower lockers filled up with 30 tins of plums, 40 tins of peaches, 20 tins of pears, two tins of prunes, and so on to a total of 120 tins of fruit. I do love fruit, but there was no possibility of eating my way through 120 tins in 28 days. But I could not decide which type of fruit to cut down. On my last crossing I had been possessed of a mad desire for peaches and it had proved to be such an obsession that I had been forced to ration myself to half a tin a day, a great hardship when one has little willpower and much appetite. If possible I wanted to avoid a similar shortage, but could not decide which fruit would prove to be my passion. Would it be peaches again? Or plums? There were strong indications it was going to be plums, but the matter was by no means certain so, rather than risk it, I left the 120 tins of fruit where they were, in the lockers already crammed with tins of vegetables, fruit juice, and savories.

"*Merde alors!* What's all this?" exclaimed Jacques, on discovering the bulging lockers. And I was forced to explain that this large number of tins was essential to counterbalance the weight of the heavy new batteries to port.

Each tin had to have its label removed before the bilge water did the job instead and each had to be marked with its contents in waterproof ink. I never used a code in case I should lose the key, but made do with abbreviations instead. Thus apple-and-raspberry pie filling became "Ap & Rasp," while green peppers filled with rice and vegetables became "stffd peps."

In the midst of stowing the large quantities of food, Mother and Father arrived to give a helping hand. Since Mother never traveled to see the family without packing a sumptuous lunch into the trunk of the car, Jacques's eyes were alight with anticipation the whole morning and little work could be done until we had consumed a large feast washed down with a bottle of wine. After which an afternoon's work didn't seem very important anyway.

"Now," said Mother, "are you taking enough food? Well, however much you think you have, I've just brought along a few extras." Whereupon she disappeared in the direction of the parking lot.

"Where's Mother?" I asked a few minutes later.

Jacques looked up and, turning pale, pointed behind me.

An enormous cardboard box was making its way ponderously along the dock and under it were Mother's legs looking uncertain around the knees. Jacques leaped to the rescue and we were soon unloading tins of artichokes, asparagus, chestnuts, rich soups, and other delicacies.

"Just a few essentials," said Mother. "Now have you got enough warm clothes?" Ever since my sister and I had left home Mother had been sure that, if we weren't underfed, we were underclothed. Having once read an advertisement about some thermal underwear "that generates its own heat" and an article about the wonders of nuclear energy on the same day, Mother was a great believer in thermonuclear underwear. Indeed, in the winter resort where my parents went skiing every year, Mother was famous for her thermonuclear underwear, which she swore, defied any number of sudden sittings in the snow.

Having given me a full set of her special underwear, Mother triumphantly held up a string of paper panties. "Much more practical," she declared. "Although I've brought a small bag of detergent and some clothespins as well, just in case you have the time."

The paper panties and warm underwear were packed into polyethylene bags with some other clothes and stowed into side lockers, which Jacques had specially built to give me extra space. He knew that, much as I may declare I was going to travel light, I always seemed to carry clothing for six months. Just as I worried about not having enough plums to eat, so I hated the thought of arriving in Newport without exactly the right thing to wear for every conceivable occasion. For the crossing itself I had gathered six complete changes of warm clothes so that, with a bit of luck, I would have enough dry clothes to last till Newport. I thought of packing each complete change separately, but for simplicity decided to put all thick sweaters in one polyethylene bag, all jeans in another, all vests in another, and so on. It was another decision I was to very much regret.

While Mother helped stow food and clothing, Father inspected the boat with Jacques. This consisted of shaking the rigging, examining the new tiller, and generally glaring at all the fittings that could possibly break. After looking through the tool bag to make sure it was equipped with the right number of wrenches, grips, vises, and cutting implements, he finally grunted his approval and disappeared into a locker to grapple with a troublesome fuel valve.

In the final week before we had to leave for Plymouth, I hurried off to the Meteorological Office at Bracknell to find out if the North Atlantic promised any unusual conditions that year. I had phoned for an appointment with Arthur Blackham in the Ships Routeing Section and had been surprised to find my name produced an immediate response.

"I know you," he declared, "you're the one with the father who phones every day." At first I thought he had me confused with the daughter of a fanatical gardener, but Arthur's memory had stretched back three years to my previous crossing when, unknown to me, Father had phoned for weather news daily. Arthur quickly assured me that this had been no bother at all. On the contrary, he was glad to have been able to reassure Father as to the lack of gales, hurricanes, and other such unpleasant events.

"Glad to do it again this time," said Arthur as we pored over current and wind charts. "You shouldn't have any gales around the Azores."

"I'm not going that way," I mentioned.

"You're . . . " he stared at me aghast. " Not the northern route! Well, I hope your boat is capable of withstanding Force 8." He paused thoughtfully. "No, I'll rephrase that — Force 9."

I couldn't help thinking Arthur was being a bit pessimistic, but then I remembered that, as a master mariner, he had crossed the Atlantic a few more times than I had.

"But it's a very good year for icebergs," he continued, which I rightly took to mean that there weren't very many. On the last race, four years before, there had been many hundreds in the path of the direct route, But this year there were only 30 large bergs in thousands of square miles of ocean. "That's good?" I asked. "That's marvelous," affirmed Arthur. "It would need the luck of the devil to hit one this year!"

I was to remind him of that statement.

With a final check to make sure I hadn't forgotten the sextant, spare sextant, navigation tables, charts, ship's papers, passport with U.S. visa, medical kit, face cream, spare tin opener, and the thousand and one other things to remember, Jacques and I set sail for Plymouth. It was a wonderful sail, but with only a week to go before the start I was beginning to feel nervous and I spent most of the time puttering about the boat wondering what I had forgotten to do. Jacques kept reassuring me that preparation was 90 percent of the Transatlantic Race and that I would be one of the few to be fully prepared. "I mean, what have you got left on your list of things to do?" he asked. I looked down the list and read out a few items like "Buy small tin of face cream for Panic Bag." "There you are," said Jacques, "you're hardly prepared at all!"

Millbay Docks at Plymouth were already full of boats, and more were arriving by the hour. The final number of entries had dropped to about 120 but, seen in a mass, it still seemed an awful lot. The French had the most impressive fleet of boats. They had dominated the race for many years and were determined to be first again in Newport.

The race was divided into three classes: the Jester Class for small boats under 38 feet, the Gipsy Moth Class for intermediate sizes, and the Pen Duick Class for the giants more than 65 feet. Most of the very large boats were French because, theoretically at least, the larger the boat the faster it goes, and the French were determined to be the fastest. *Club Méditerranée* had arrived and was ready to start, although this was hard to believe from the many workers swarming over her decks. If anything she was larger than I had imagined and I could only stare in awe at her four tall masts with their enormous sail area. If one person had to sail that ship singlehanded I was extremely grateful it wasn't going to be me.

Tucked away among the throng of boats were several I knew well from the Round Britain and Azores races. Significantly most of them were moored in a line together and, while other competitors scurried around looking worried, these boats echoed to the sound of laughter and clinking glasses. If there had been a prize for enjoying the prerace week, the British would certainly have won it, followed closely by the Czech, Polish, and Dutch contingents whose day seemed to start at 11 P.M. As always the attitude of the British left the French perplexed and confused. Was this the great British challenge, out to regain their lost trophies? Surely, in the wake of Francis Chichester and Geoffrey Williams, previous British winners of the race, didn't we want to win again? But for most people the short answer was no, unless by some delightful stroke of fate one just happened to arrive first. It was the British attitude that the racing mustn't interfere with the main purpose of the adventure, which was to have an enjoyable time in Plymouth, make one's way across the Atlantic in a reasonably seamanlike manner without taking too long about it, and to have an even more delightful time in Newport by way of recovery. It was the getting there that was important rather than the time one took to do it. Not to say that everyone didn't have a passage time he was hoping to match or better. But then, if one had taken 60 or even 80 days on the previous race, this didn't take much doing. The secret of the British nonchallenge lay in their choice of boats. While the French glittered in an array of light, fast, and fantastic racing machines, the British glowed quietly in a jumbled collection of standard family cruising boats and unusual ocean craft designed for seaworthiness rather than speed.

There were exceptions, the most notable being Mike McMullen's *Three Cheers*, which was the only British entry with a chance of being first in Newport. Mike and his yellow trimaran had very nearly won the Round Britain Race, losing the 2,000 mile race by only one hour, and we were certain he could win the Transatlantic. *Three Cheers* was only 46 feet long but she was very light and fast. With the help of his fabulous wife, Lizzie, Mike had worked immensely hard on the boat, always sailing and tuning her in search of more speed. Even in the first days of that week in Plymouth, Mike forwent the reunion parties to take *Three Cheers* sailing. But we were all behind him, not only because he was such a trier, but because he managed to combine determination with a tremendous sense of fun.

Sometimes it was nice to dream of speeding along at 20 knots in a boat like *Three Cheers*, but there were other boats that made us envious and for entirely different reasons. The craft that made us almost speechless with jealousy was Jock Macleod's *Ron Glas*. Jock was a chap who liked his sailing. But he also liked his comfort and failed to see why one should always preclude the other as seemed to be the rule. He had commissioned Angus Primrose to design him a "gentleman's boat" that would sail adequately but not in such a manner as to get one wet. The result was the junk-rigged schooner *Ron Glas*.

The essence of the junk rig is that it can be entirely controlled from a remote position. In the case of *Ron Glas*, all sailhoisting, trimming, and reefing were "handled" from the cockpit. Since the cockpit could be completely enclosed and boasted a swivel armchair, this meant that Jock could sit back in the warm and dry, a glass of Scotch at his elbow, and sail for thousands of miles without venturing on deck. This bore such favorable comparison with sail changing on the heaving and very wet foredeck of a conventional yacht that *Ron Glas* was always full of visitors eyeing her design with wonder and delight. Even those of us who knew the boat well couldn't help feeling a renewed pang of envy at the sight of Jock's oilskins still as bright and unsalty as the day he had bought them, and there was a strong rumor that in all the years Jock had been sailing the boat, he had never once put them on.

40

The keen racing boys were always trying to find ways of saving weight in order to go faster, but Jock's priorities were somewhat different.

"What's the boat's water capacity, Jock?" asked an interested visitor.

"A hundred gallons," replied Jock.

"And how much are you taking on the race?"

"A hundred gallons."

"But that's going to weigh you down, isn't it?"

"Well yes," agreed Jock, "but then I've got to have enough to use my shower. And of course, enough to get me back to Scotland after the race."

"But can't you fill up with water in Newport?"

"Why no!" exclaimed Jock, looking shocked. "It's full of chlorine and would quite ruin my Scotch and water."

Another Angus Primrose junk-rigged design was the famous *Galway Blazer* that Bill King had sailed around the world singlehanded. It was now owned by Peter Crowther who held the transatlantic record for the slowest crossing ever. In the last race Peter had sailed an old gaffer called *Golden Vanity* and taken 80 days to reach Newport. Luckily his food and water had held out although it had been touch and go for, unbeknown to him, his cat had also been attending a few parties in Plymouth and gave birth to a fine litter in the middle of the Atlantic. The kittens were in good health on arrival, though Peter was beginning to look decidedly skinny.

But the best-known junk-rigged boat of all was *Jester*. This fine little boat had taken part in every race so far, first belonging to the race's originator, Blondie Hasler, and then to the capable Mike Richey. Mike was an expert navigator and a director of the Institute of Navigation, but during the last race, he had not been so expert in his provisioning and, so the story went, had begun to run short of whiskey while still miles from Newport. He was understandably delighted therefore when a ship stopped and lowered a bottle attached to a life buoy. Anticipation mounting, Mike waited patiently for the bottle to float over. Then, catching it at last, he whipped it out of the water only to find the bottle was quite empty save for a scrap of paper with his position on it.

Few boat designers seem to take their own boats on long ocean crossings, but Angus Primrose was different. Having seen so many of his designs go around the world or across the Atlantic singlehanded, he had decided to take one of his standard production boats in both the Azores and the Transatlantic races. The boat Angus had chosen was a beamy family cruising boat that he affectionately referred to as "the block of flats" because of its high topsides and large amount of accommodation. Significantly, its cockpit could seat more people with drinks in their hands than boats of twice its size, and frequently did. Angus had done very well in the light airs of the Azores Race and took enormous delight in telling everyone what a relaxed race he had had.

"Three meals a day, eight hours sleep a night, and only changed sail twice. Nothing to this singlehanding," he said. That remark cost him a lot of drinks, but Angus never minded and would merely repeat it with undiminished glee.

In Plymouth, Angus was not his usual cheerful self. Apparently he was having a bit of trouble with the Customs about the matter of bonded stores. He had put in a perfectly reasonable request for six cases of duty-free Scotch, just about enough for the crossing and a few parties in Newport afterward, but he was horrified to find that the Customs were doing all kinds of unnecessary sums, like a third of a bottle a day multiplied by 40 days equaled only thirteen bottles. Angus pointed out that he might take 50 days, even 60, and it'd be a pretty poor situation if the boat ran dry. Nobody was certain how the problem was solved, but solved it must have been for after a couple of days the grin reappeared on Angus's face.

Among other old friends in the race was Martin Wills who held the record for the second slowest crossing of the Atlantic. Martin only bothered to keep his boat sailing if the wind was being what he described as "reasonable." If it blew anything remotely "unreasonable" he was inclined to lower all sail and read one of the many hundreds of comics with which he stocked the boat, getting under way again only when he remembered to, if then.

Two other old friends were Richard Clifford in *Shamaal* and Gustaf Versluys in *Tyfoon,* both of whom had been great friends and rivals in the Round Britain. Gustaf, who was the friendliest of teddy bears and quite the best thing to come out of Belgium since brussels sprouts, had the 35-foot Ohlson, younger sister to the *Golly*. But having the smaller boat was no problem to Gustaf; one look at the size of his shoulders and I knew he wouldn't be far behind me, not to say very far in front.

It was marvelous to see so many old friends, but as the week progressed I had to spend more and more time on the *Golly* trying to sort out the last-minute problems and panics. Luckily for me, it was Jacques's half-term holiday and he was able to stay down for the whole week. Without him nothing at all would have got done, for every time I started to do a job another reporter would appear for an interview. Most were very polite, offering to come back later if I was busy, but others always seemed to have a deadline they were about to miss and couldn't wait a second. Most of their questions were good but there were a fair number of, "Why does a nice girl like you . . . .?" By far the most popular was, "are you expecting a rough trip?" which was a bit masochistic, I decided. After a lot of thought I came up with what I considered to be a reasonable but not unlucky reply, and it was really vital not to say anything unlucky. It's not that I'm superstitious but I do think it must be tempting fate to say, "Rough trip? No, no, I'm expecting lovely weather." So I hit upon the reply "I'm expecting gales for the first half of the trip and fog for the second and then I won't be disappointed!" which I thought covered the situation quite nicely without being too pessimistic. At least, that was what I believed then.

The only question I found impossible to answer was, "But how do you manage a large boat like this?" Quite clearly I could manage her, otherwise I wouldn't be there, but I was up against the image of the singlehanded lady sailor. If you were anything short of being a nautical lady wrestler, then you were too weak to handle anything more than a dinghy. I became a little tired of this and started to behave badly when the question came up. I would give a good imitation of Charles Atlas in one of his more amazing poses or stride up to the questioner and give him a hearty slap on the back while offering, in ringing tones, to show him my biceps if he could spare me a moment.

About one thing I was certain: On being asked when I hoped to arrive in Newport, I answered with great certainty, "July the fourth." This would mean making the crossing in 28 days, which was a fast time. "So you're out to win the lady's prize and beat the lady's record!" whistled a reporter, writing busily. Certainly both those things would be nice but I didn't bother to explain the more important reason for arriving then. If I arrived any later I would have less than a week to spend with Jacques and my parents before they had to return to England. Also the Fourth of July marked the 200th anniversary of American Independence and I didn't want to miss the celebrations. Besides the whole point of taking the *Golly* was to get there in a faster time than my previous five and a half weeks, which had seemed far too long. Four weeks would be a great improvement and, although it would mean averaging 100 miles a day, I was sure the *Golly* could do it.

Although I had seen them at a distance I hadn't had a chance to meet the other girls in the race until one of the *Observer* photographers decided we must get together for a group photograph. The poor fellow should have known better than to try to assemble a group of women, albeit only four. Every time he herded three of us together the fourth would be faced by some awful crisis and unable to attend. This fourth would usually be the marvelous Ida who would rush off and issue a torrent of Italian at some failed instrument or another. But she finally appeared wreathed in smiles, and in the same place at the same time as the rest of us. It was a remarkable feat and, since it had taken two days to achieve, the photographer was almost beside himself with excitement and dropped his camera.

Although our conversation was limited to repeated cries of "Good Luck!" due to language difficulties, the four of us became firm friends, united by the pioneering spirit of women putting to sea — and the knowledge that we were outnumbered by men 30 to 1. But at least we had taken the opportunity to meet each other, and that was more than could be said for most of the fleet. This, for me, was the sad part of having such a large number of boats. There just wasn't the time for everyone to get to know each other. However, there was a feeling of comradeship not always found in other sailing events. Tools and spares were lent with spontaneity and information exchanged with eagerness.

The week progressed in an uncoordinated but happy way until Wednesday when we heard dreadful news. The lovely Lizzie McMullen had died. She had been killed by an electric sander that had fallen in the water as she helped Mike to polish the bottom of *Three Cheers*. Lizzie had been much loved by those who knew her, and her death created great sadness. For some of us, this terrible accident cast a shadow over the race that was never to disappear.

By the end of the week everyone had clubbed together to provide the most magnificent trophy — the Lizzie McMullen Memorial Trophy for the first multihull to finish. There was little doubt that Mike himself would win it if he decided to continue with the race. It must have been an impossible decision for him, but in the end Mike took what we all firmly believed to be the right one. He decided to go ahead. The two of them had worked so hard and so long toward the race that he was sure Lizzie would have wanted him to participate. Also sailing singlehanded keeps one very busy, while an empty house permits time for thought.

In the last two days the *Golly* became increasingly full of people and unstowed gear. The BBC technical team arrived with the cameras I was to take for "The World About Us." They also arrived with tape recorders, remote controls, and miles and miles of wire. I was absolutely horrified. Where were my easy-to-use cameras with built-in sound? I was told that they had proved to be unsuitable, but no one had happened to mention this to me. Instead there was all this equipment that looked very complicated and, I was miserable to find, *was* so.

"All you have to do," said the BBC man, "is load the film in here, close the waterproof case . . . oh, and push this switch here . . . which is a bit inaccessible, isn't it? But then you just pop the camera on its bracket on the stern, bring the wire back here to the remote switch . . ." He drew a long breath. "Then load the tape recorder, activate it by pushing these switches here . . . run *its* lead back to the remote switch and . . . . ah yes, the microphone. Now that runs from here to you . . . ." By this time the boat was covered in leads, switches, and miscellaneous equipment, and I viewed it with mounting anxiety.

"*Finally*," said the BBC man, taking a last breath, "there's the sound synchronization. Now when you have everything running if you could just say 'Roll Three' or whatever, hold up three fingers . . ." — I noticed he hadn't used Roll Two as an example — "and then clap your hands, careful to make sure the noise is picked up by the microphone." So I was to be a human clapboard. If this wasn't enough to silence me I was finally made speechless by the arrival of several large boxes of unexposed film, tape cassettes, and batteries to run the cameras and recorders. All the stowage having been taken up with food, clothing, and other bulky matter, it was a difficult job to find room for it and, in the end, the film and tapes had to cohabit with five pounds of apples and a bunch of bananas.

I looked carefully at the BBC technician and wondered if he had the slightest idea of what he was asking me to do, decided he didn't and that it was hopeless to ask for some simpler equipment at this late stage. My only consolation was the memory of this same technician jumping off the *Golly's* bows into the water some months before. The only question was whether the water had been cold enough.

On Thursday there was a mass arrival — Mother and Father, Ron and Joan with three of their children, and a send-off party from the Chichester Yacht Club under whose burgee the *Golly* sailed. Everyone offered to help and rushed off in various directions on unknown errands. But Mother and Joan did a fine job with the fresh food shopping, patiently searching out unripe fruit and vegetables and some Scottish oatcakes for which I had a sudden yen. But there was one thing that we could not find in Plymouth and that was whole meal bread. Although I am a great lover of natural food, this was not the only reason for finding this particular bread. Whole meal bread is the only kind that stays fresh for weeks, and though I had the means to bake fresh bread on the passage, it is a lot of work and would be impossible in bad weather. But Plymouth proudly offered us brown, whole wheat, rye, granary, and a variety of other breads, everything but whole meal. Finally we had to send an SOS to my press agent, Margot, who was coming down from London the next day, asking her to bring ten small whole meal loaves or five large. Margot, anxious not to fall down on her mission, staggered onto the train with twelve small loaves and four large, which cleared out one small bakery in the region of London's St. John's Wood.

One very important purchase was my All Bran, without which my day came to a terrible halt. As every connoisseur knows there is nothing worse than soggy All Bran, so it had to be bought at the last minute, divided into small quantities, and wrapped in polyethylene bags before stowing. On my last Atlantic trip All Bran had been the last thing I needed, but I wasn't sure if this had resulted from being at sea or from being absolutely terrified, so I thought it best not to take many chances, and no locker could be opened without a bag of All Bran falling out and bursting over the floor.

"Now, darling, you cannot possibly go without *this!*" said

Mother, pressing a small bottle of tablets into my hand. They were what was commonly known in the family as Mother's All-Purpose Pills. Nobody was allowed to travel without them, particularly to countries where water was less than pure. And although the pills were designed to combat the dreaded "continental tummy," they were also brought into action against aching heads, unsteady limbs, and hangovers in general which, against all the evidence, Mother would nobly declare to be the beginnings of the dreaded Lurgy itself.

"And," said Mother conspiratorially, "I've just brought you a few little extras." The extras were more tins of asparagus, artichokes, chestnuts, and delicate soups, which I stowed with the others in my Treats Locker. Into the same locker Jacques slipped a few mysterious packets with the strict instructions that I was not to look at them until several days after the start. And there was a parcel from my godmother, Roma, with the message "Not to Be Opened Until One Week Out," heavily underlined in threatening black ink. And there were many other gifts: bottles of champagne, books, and good luck charms. Although there was one lucky charm that I instinctively felt to be unlucky and quietly removed from the boat. The boat already had a mascot, of course, and not surprisingly this was the Robertson's symbol, a "golly." He lived up above the radio where he could survey the whole cabin. But he was now joined by several miniature gollies, an owl, many colorful good luck cards, and countless telegrams. If good wishes could make a boat lucky, then the *Golly* must be.

Jack Hill came down on the Friday to write the first piece about me for the *Express* and we went through all the details of our radio schedules to make sure we had covered everything. I also made a radio date with Ron and Joan who were to travel to America on the *QE2*, passing within a hundred miles of the track I hoped to take.

Jacques and I spent Friday evening over a quiet family supper and then slipped away for an early night at a hotel.

From the hotel window I looked down at the lights of Plymouth, bright and full of life, and out toward Plymouth Sound where ships lay at anchor, their riding lights twinkling across the dark water, and then beyond, to where the Eddystone Light flashed in the middle of the black open sea. I tried to imagine being out there with 3,000 miles of ocean ahead and no Jacques to help.

"You know, I'm sure there's enough food on that boat for a stowaway as well," I said. "How about disguising yourself as a sailbag?"

"Mmmm," murmured Jacques thoughtfully," I could leave a plastic replica of myself in the classroom. But I'm afraid the children might never notice the difference."

4

"You'll put on your safety harness now and then, won't you?" said Father, trying not to look anxious.

"And do remember to eat . . . and wrap up well," added Mother, giving me a fierce look through damp eyes.

"You'll win, just you wait and see!" cried the ever-unquenchable Ron with a madly waving Joan at his side.

As the boat moved away from the dock I gave them my most dazzling and confident smile, then turned quickly away before I should do anything so un-British as to burst into tears. Jacques, who was staying aboard until I was safely out and under way, secured the line from the towing launch and we moved out into the Sound. We tied on behind one of the anchored boats from the Chichester Yacht Club and started to prepare the *Golly* for sea.

Those hours waiting to move up to the start were the worst. When I thought of the race I felt sick with excitement and apprehension, and when I thought of my family I was miserable, not only at having to say good-bye, but at subjecting them to so much worry and uncertainty. After all the months of preparation the start would be an enormous relief for me and I would be able to forget everything except the sailing of the boat; but for Jacques and my parents it would be the beginning of an anxious four weeks.

As we waited through that long morning my brain became more and more addled and I kept repeating the same reminders to Jacques. "*Do* tell Mum and Dad the radio could easily break down and that silence doesn't mean disaster." Every time I said it, Jacques would reassure me with a hug and a few words of encouragement, only to repeat a few reminders of his own about wearing a safety harness, and not knocking my head although, he added, it might do it some good, and about eating, and wrapping up, and a few hundred other things.

At last it was time to sail up toward the line just outside Plymouth Sound. As we rounded Drake's Island my heart sank at the sight of the motor boat that was to take Jacques away and I became very un-British indeed, clinging to him like a barnacle as the tears ran down my cheeks. Then he was gone and I had to remind myself that I was doing all this for fun. My face uncrumpled a bit and I kept a look out for all the spectator boats that were milling about. There were about a thousand of them in addition to the hundred or more competitors trying to maneuver their craft singlehanded. Fortunately the wind was light and no one was going too fast, so we could avoid each other with time to spare. As we waited near the line, competitors exchanged waves and shouts of "I'll have a drink waiting for you in Newport" to which would come the reply, "No, *I'll* have a drink waiting for *you!*" But more often it was just a wave and a "Good Luck."

The Pen Duick class was to start first and this was much appreciated by the smaller boats who did not rate their chances under the bows of *Club Med*. The Gipsy Moth Class was to follow half an hour later and finally the Jester Class, the largest with well over 60 boats.

When the starting gun for the large boats sounded you could almost feel the relief run through the rest of the fleet.

Won't be seeing you again till Newport, I thought as they sailed slowly away, and it was a perfectly reasonable thing to believe at the time. Next came the intermediate class, immediately led by the bright yellow *Three Cheers* in hot pursuit of the larger boats. Then it was our turn at last. Starting well doesn't really matter on a long race so I had no intention of making a hot departure. But I was unhappy to find that I was early at the line and quickly turned away to run down the length of it. This meant I was facing the wrong way when the gun finally went and it took me some time to get the boat on course and sailing. Not a very organized beginning to my race and not a very fortunate one either. Unknown to me I had incurred a large time penalty for being over the line five seconds before the start.

The relief at being under way was marvelous. I checked the sail trim, tidied up a few lines, and settled back to enjoy the sensation of sailing again, although the normal peace and quiet were notably absent. There were helicopters buzzing overhead and spectator boats swooping about among the competitors, wishing everyone good luck. And then there was the unmistakable sound of Ron's voice shouting, "marvelous," "arrive in no time," and "open another bottle of champagne immediately." My parents were there on the same boat as Ron and Joan, and they followed me for an hour, waving and smiling and toasting me with champagne at frequent intervals. It was nice to know that, even if Mother and Father were anxious and worried, they must be feeling less so every minute.

But I could see no sign of Jacques. Though I had been looking out for him continually, I had not seen him since he had disappeared in the motor boat. A last wave would have been nice but, as the spectator boats thinned out and the little motor boat was nowhere to be seen, I realized it must have turned back a long time before. With a last wave and cheer of encouragement the champagne special also turned away, and I felt a bit lonely.

I sailed out to sea for another hour, then tacked toward the west and the Lizard. The fleet had already dispersed to an amazing extent and I could count only about 20 boats, although there were still a few nearby including Aline Marchand, one of the French girls. But as the wind dropped to a light breeze, Aline and several others passed me by. It was no surprise; the *Golly* hated light airs, and if there was to be a lot of light weather ahead, we would be passed by many more boats. But it didn't bother me too much. As a young and keen dinghy sailor I had wanted to win every race I entered, but now I was a bit more philosophical. For one thing there was absolutely nothing I could do about the weather and that, with the route I chose, would decide how well I would do. For another thing, I didn't want to push the boat too hard and risk breaking a vital piece of gear. More than anything, I wanted to arrive safely. It would mean sacrificing speed, but I considered it a very small price to pay for the sight of Newport.

But here I was dreaming of arriving and I had hardly left. That, I decided, wouldn't do at all. I was as bad as the sailors of old who were always longing to return to sea and, once they were afloat again, dreamed only of reaching harbor. It was much better to look just one or two days ahead and not anticipate too much. In that way I would not be disappointed if the crossing took me a long time. Although with a bit of luck. . . . For luck I had a St. Christopher medal that always hung around my neck. Not that I was superstitious of course. It was just that I felt uncomfortable without that medallion and never took it off.

After the excitement of the start I felt completely drained of energy. Like a sack of potatoes I sat in the cockpit, staring vacantly into space for hour after hour. I had experienced this kind of apathy after starting races before and knew that I should make a valiant effort to overcome it, but it flowed over me like a warm blanket and I was too weak to resist. Being in a woozy state didn't matter too much except that it played havoc with my navigation. I had a vague idea of my compass heading because the compass was right in front of me, but I had taken no distance readings from the log, so when, at long last, I pried my bottom off the seat and went down to plot my position, it was, to say the least, approximate. If we had been heading into the open sea it wouldn't have mattered a bit, but I had to find my way around the Lizard, which would invariably have shrouded itself in fog whenever I approached, and then around the Scillies, which would doubtless follow suit and disappear in mist.

I felt reasonably confident that I was heading toward the Lizard, more or less, and in the late afternoon I was delighted to see the headland appear straight ahead. This was marvelous, for it meant that I would pass it on a favorable tide and be well clear of the heavy shipping by morning. With the coming of dusk a mist started to form and, as the visibility dropped, I waited anxiously for the Lizard light to come on and indicate the position of the headland. At last I saw the powerful flashes through the gathering gray and sighed with relief. No problems now. Good old Lizard, flashing every three seconds. I spun around and looked again in horror. The light was no more flashing than I was! It was most definitely occulting. I groaned and clutched my head in dismay. How could I have been so stupid? It was St. Anthony's Head, the headland in front of Falmouth, and if I'd taken the remotest trouble over my navigation, I would have realized that several hours ago.

What a great start to the race — 30 miles out and totally lost. It was obviously time to take myself in hand so I gave myself a firm talking to. This mainly consisted of striding up and down the cockpit muttering "Absolutely marvelous, what a great navigator you are!" and "Couldn't find London if you were motoring down the Thames!" Suitably chastened, I turned my attention to finding the real Lizard, which was about 15 miles to the southwest. A 15-mile error in 30, that wasn't bad I thought bitterly. Normally I prided myself on my navigation, but at that degree of error I would find myself not in Newport, Rhode Island, but in Nova Porto, Argentina. The only consolation was that, in working back over my navigation and doing it properly, it was obvious that I must be somewhere near Falmouth. Also sleepiness and apathy were a form of seasickness I often experienced and, had I not been suffering from it, I would doubtless have taken my usual care. That's what I persuaded myself anyway.

True to form the Lizard shrouded itself in fog as I approached and by the time I arrived there with what seemed to be the entire fleet, we only had the loud "Whroom" of the siren to guide us around. I can think of nicer ways to spend the first night of a long race than tacking around a headland with a hundred other boats in swirling mist, and as if to illustrate just what a daunting experience it can be, I was horrified to see the enormous shape of a giant yacht looming out of the mist on the opposite tack. I happened to be on starboard, which gave me right-of-way but there are times when one presses these matters and times when one retires gracefully. This was one of the times for retreat and I tacked away hoping that it was finally and definitely the last time I would see any of the large yachts. As I sailed off I was very impressed to hear the unmistakable sounds of the giant boat tacking. So he had given way to me after all. But I couldn't help feeling sorry for him as the sounds of screaming winches, flapping sails, and general confusion went on for a good five minutes. Compared to that, tacking the *Golly* must be easy.

At three in the morning I found myself abreast of the Lizard on a fair tide and with improving visibility. I could see the light clearly (and I knew it was the right light because I had timed its three-second flashes at least five times). In the illumination of its beam I could also see the cliffs beneath and the silhouette of a yacht. But there was something awfully wrong; unless I was mistaken, the yacht was heading directly for the rocks. This was not time for a nice sleep, but I feared that somebody was having a really good snore. There was nothing I could do and I watched with growing anxiety as the boat edged nearer and nearer the towering light. Disaster seemed inevitable and I was about to call the coast guard when the yacht suddenly turned away. From the rapidity of the turn and the quite opposite course that the yacht took I guessed that somebody had given himself a severe shock, though I never discovered who it was.

For me there was no sleep. It was too risky near land and shipping, particularly when the visibility was bad. But I managed to stay awake all that night and much of the following day without feeling too many ill effects. Not to say there weren't bad patches. The worst was around dawn when my body began to realize that the night was nearly over and there was still no likelihood of being allowed any sleep. As the daylight filtered through the mist my eyelids grew lead weights and my chin dropped onto my chest every few minutes. I would wake with a start unable, for a moment, to imagine where I was. I slept for only a second at a time but in that moment a beautiful vision would leap into my imagination. It was always the same. I would be there in the cockpit and someone, usually Jacques, would appear from the hatch and in a warm comforting voice say, "You can go and sleep now. It's my watch." I would be just on the point of going below when to my disgust I would wake up again and find myself quite alone.

Every few minutes I would take a long look around, although there was rarely anything to see but a white blanket. But suddenly I saw a shape emerge from the mist about a mile away to port. Oh no! It was *Club Méditerranée* again! I was beginning to wonder if the large boats would ever forge ahead as they were meant to do. But for the moment at least *Club Med* obliged by overhauling me slowly and disappearing in the direction of the Atlantic. He was followed shortly by another large boat, the 70-foot catamaran *Kriter III*. I was beginning to realize that these large boats were not as fast as they were cracked up to be. If I could stay ahead of them for 18 hours, then other boats should be able to do so for very much longer. It was going to be a very interesting race.

Gales may be unpleasant, but calms provide the most trying conditions when you are singlehanded. And now the wind was dying away with every minute. My heart sank; I had been hoping to be out past the Scillies by nightfall, but now I was faced with another 24 hours in the thick of the shipping with no sleep. As if to stress the importance of staying awake I heard the throb of distant engines on several occasions. Once, some engines seemed to be coming quite close, and peering anxiously through the mist, I finally spotted a ship heading toward me. If it had been a Greek tanker I would unhesitatingly have broken the seal that the race officials had so carefully put on my gear lever and motored like a fiend in the opposite direction. But seeing that the ship was a minesweeper and in all likelihood British, I was filled with a confidence that was soon justified by the vessel altering course to a pass around me. And, despite my tiredness, I couldn't help feeling a glow of pleasure as men appeared from all over the ship to cheer and wave. I had a strong suspicion they were aware that the entire British ladies' team was waving back at them.

The trouble with light winds is that the self-steering doesn't work well, if at all. And there's something about sailing back in the direction from whence one's come that I find infinitely depressing, even if I'm only doing it at an eighth of a knot. Some self-steering gears will send their boats in small circles but mine specialized in pointing me on a reciprocal course to the one I wished to take. This was very frustrating, so rather than head back to England, I hand steered the *Golly* westward, alternately nodding off and singing to keep myself awake. My singing is nothing to be proud of and would prevent any music lover from sleeping, but it always seemed to fail with me, possibly because one can get used to anything.

But at last a small breeze came up and, after a few false starts, established itself from the southwest, blowing the mist away as it strengthened. Soon the sun was shining out of a blue sky and sparkling on the water like silver. I could see Land's End away to starboard and Wolf Rock to port, the visibility as brilliant as it had been poor an hour before. I set course for the Seven Stones Lightship to the north of the Scillies, trimmed the sails, and felt the *Golly* pulling steadily through the water.

What a marvelous sailing day. The *Golly* sped along in the beam wind, steady as a rock in the flat sea, while the sun shone brightly overhead. Of course it wasn't very warm, and certainly not warm enough to tear off my clothes and start getting that deep and luxurious tan I'd been promising myself, but there'd be plenty of time for that. Or I hoped there would be. I'd brought four tubes of suntan lotion, two pairs of dark glasses, and a book on transcendental meditation with which to cover my face.

Although I was still in the shipping lanes I felt the visibility was good enough to risk some short snatches of sleep. Ten minutes is not very much, and nothing compared to the lovely eight hours I dreamed about, but these catnaps were surprisingly refreshing and after three or four I felt sufficiently awake to do some chores. I tidied up the cockpit, coiling up the many sheets and halyards that ran back to it, then sluiced out the last of the dirt and grit that had accumulated on the cockpit floor. I cleaned the galley and reorganized the icebox so that, as the ice melted, the milk, yogurt, and cold drinks would not fall over and spill. And then I eyed the washing up. I had eaten very little since the previous day, just some fruit and cheese, a hot drink, and some *muesli* for breakfast, and yet a surprising amount of dishes, knives, and forks had gathered in the washing-up bucket. This bucket sat in the cockpit and gave me an accusing look every time I stepped over it, so I filled it with seawater and resolved to settle down and tackle it the very next time I passed. Some hours later I was surprised to see the bucket was as full as it had been before. Goodness, hadn't I done that? I examined the contents more closely. It seemed to me that the motion of the boat was swilling the water around and over the dishes astonishingly effectively; in another hour or two everything would doubtless be clean as a whistle, apart, perhaps, from those few stubborn bits. I stepped over the bucket and made a firm mental note to finish the job the very next time I passed.

The one chore that was no chore at all was my first radio call to Jack Hill. I looked forward to it all morning and warmed up the set well in advance to be sure of getting through on time. I was still far too close to Portishead Radio, a long-range station that used high-frequency transmissions, to have any hope of getting through. So on this one occasion I would call Jack through Land's End Radio, one of the string of coast stations that operated with a range of a few hundred miles. Although I had used the set several times since its installation, I was still a little nervous and, having selected the right frequencies and tuned them in, I called with some hesitancy. Three quarters of an hour later I was shouting down the radio. I could get no response at all from Land's End and it was already 15 minutes past the 12 o'clock date I had fixed with Jack. Now and then I could hear Land's End talking on their working frequencies, but they did not seem to hear me on the calling frequency, and I grew increasingly worried in case the radio was faulty. To make matters worse I knew Jacques would be there at Jack's house, waiting and worrying too. But at long last, just as I was getting desperate, they answered my call. It was clear that they had no trouble in receiving me and I could not understand why they had not answered before. Possibly they were busy, but I had heard little traffic in progress, and the matter remained a mystery.

The waiting was over and I was soon hearing the voices of the two J's, the one asking if I was all right and taking care and the other demanding to know if I was feeling OK, being careful, eating well, and not feeling too tired. After giving them my position and my news, and frequent reassurances as to my health and safety, I then elicited from Jacques that yes, he would eat well, and take care on the roads and remember to water the vegetables and pump up the slow puncture on my car. And, most important of all, find out why the U.S. Embassy hadn't sent his visa yet. By the time we were all sufficiently reassured as to each other's safety and well-being, I was worried about flattening the batteries, not to mention hitting the Seven Stones Lightship, which was somewhere just ahead, and reluctantly said good-bye.

There was one more chore to do before I could snatch some sleep, and that was the filming for the BBC. I had decided to take a roll of film every day, which would provide them with about 30 rolls out of the 50 or 60 they had given me. Each roll was only three and a half minutes long, so I did not think it would be too difficult to find enough things to say, but to be on the safe side I made a list of topics to use. Now all I had to do was to set the whole thing up. It really couldn't be as complicated as it had looked in Plymouth and I felt quite cheerful as I assembled the various pieces of equipment from around the boat. Ten minutes later I was sitting in a mass of tangled wires, the camera whirring without permission, and the microphone hanging upside down around my knees.

Undeterred I started again. This time I managed to un-tangle the wires and start the camera on command, but, having spoken my commentary with what I confidently felt to be quiet fascination interspersed with brilliant zest, I then discovered I had forgotten to turn on the tape recorder. Loading the camera with yet another cassette of film, I faced the lens again, yelled "Roll One," held up one finger, and clapped my hands. This time I was sure I had everything right and embarked on my commentary with renewed confidence. Three and a half minutes turned out to be a surprisingly long time and I was a little perplexed to find out how soon my list of topics was exhausted, leaving me staring vacantly at the camera. But that, I decided, would have to do and, to be sure I had managed to record something, I wound back the tape to listen to my dazzling observations. It was a sobering experience; for two and a half minutes I listened to some strange woman talking in a strained and highly embar-rassed British voice on a variety of topics loosely connected with sailing and strung together by loud "Umms" and

"Ahs." I didn't need to count the nonsequiturs or split infinitives to know that my next career was not going to be in television.

Now at least I could sleep. I was well past the Seven Stones and clear of most of the shipping and, while there was daylight and perfect visibility, I felt it was safe to take half an hour's sleep. Just as I was preparing my sleeping bag and closing my eyes in anticipation, I had the extraordinary feeling that I was not alone. A bit early in the voyage to be showing the signs, I thought. Hadn't even started talking to myself yet. But, despite having just taken a good look around for ships and knowing there weren't any there, the feeling persisted. So I turned and made my way up the companionway, only to find myself staring into two very beady, black eyes. They belonged to a large and very cross racing pigeon. He was very cross because, try as he might, he could not balance on the lifelines and when he stopped glaring at me for long enough to try another perch, he became even more infuriated as he slipped and slithered on the shiny fiberglass. Finally he hopped into one of the small cubbyholes at the side of the cockpit where the winch handles were kept and gave me a series of threatening looks that clearly said, "I do not wish to be disturbed." Apparently we were both in need of rest and, after putting out some grain and water, I, for one, retired to my bunk and fell straight into a deep sleep.

After an afternoon of pleasant snoozing interspersed with quick looks for ships, I finally got up and considered the problem of "Pidgy." It was very nice to have such a visitor and he would doubtless become tame given enough time, but it was also certain that he would drown if he stayed aboard. We were getting farther from land all the time and soon the distance would be too great for Pidgy to cover. There would be no problem if he didn't attempt the flight, but as soon as he had rested I knew he would be off. Apart from which, he was making a terrible mess of the cubbyhole, and after reaching in to grab a winch handle on one occasion, I didn't do it again but moved the handle to a less exposed place. Every time I looked at Pidgy he was sleeping, except when I made a noise to disturb him when he would give me a ferocious glare. I decided it would not be wise to shoo him away until he had had a bit more rest.

During the night the wind went around abaft the beam and I decided to put up a spinnaker, quite forgetting that Pidgy's rest would be horribly disturbed by all the noise. By force of habit I put my hand into the cubbyhole to find the winch handle I had moved and was given a strong indication of Pidgy's feelings by receiving a sharp peck on the finger. Full of apologies I tried to keep my movements as quiet as possible and managed quite well until things got out of hand. This happens quite often with spinnakers and they must always be treated with caution. The *Golly* had an enormous spinnaker and it was a frighteningly powerful sail to cope with on my own. But the sock device that Jacques and I had fitted had taken some of the worst moments out of the setting and lowering of the sail and I approached such prickly maneuvers with a little less anxiety than before. This time I had pulled up the sail wrapped in its sock, or "the salami" as Jacques called it, set up all the guys, sheets, and poles, and then liberated the sail by hoisting the sock up the mast until it sat folded like a concertina at the top of the full sail.

So far so good, but not for long. As I admired the spinnaker in the moonlight I heard a loud whirring noise and saw the head of the sail shoot out from the masthead and, still pulling nicely, propel itself to a point about 50 feet ahead of the boat where it fell into the water with the rest of the spinnaker in hot pursuit. The spinnaker having stopped dead and the boat still traveling at seven knots, the boat soon ran over the sail and did its best to trawl it along underneath. Full of water, the sail was a terrible weight and the boat shuddered to a halt while I started on the long and exhausting job of pulling the sodden sail aboard. It was the last time I failed to make up a spinnaker halyard properly. That there were not enough cleats on the mast and I had been forced to make the halyard up over another line was some excuse, but in the future I took care to ensure there was a cleat free for the exclusive use of that powerful beastie, the large spinnaker.

After sorting out the shambles, I reset the spinnaker and we were soon off again at a roaring seven or eight knots. This was a marvelous start to the race. Instead of fighting my way through the usual wet southwesterlies here was a lovely southeasterly that was sending us out into the Atlantic and away from the shipping lanes at a fantastic rate. Even if this was the only fair wind we were to have (and it very nearly was) it couldn't have come at a better time. But it was a frightening run through that night and the next morning; *Golly* rolled and yawed from side to side as she thundered along, the spinnaker pulling harder and harder in the gathering wind. After a time the self-steering could no longer hold her and finally it became too much for me too, and I had to lower the spinnaker before the *Golly* broached once too often and something broke. Under plain sail again all was peace and order and I was able to relax and take stock. It was now noon and on plotting my noon position I was pleased to find that we had covered 145 miles in 24 hours, which was encouraging for the 100-miles-a-day average I needed to arrive by the Fourth of July.

But in all the excitement I had missed Pidgy's departure. When I went to look for him his cubbyhole was quite empty apart from the terrible mess. But though I swore at him for leaving such a lot of clearing up to be done, I was really very pleased that he had taken a good rest and then gone on his way home.

Before getting the long deep sleep I had been promising myself so long (I managed only short naps while we were tearing along under spinnaker) I had another look at the chart. By afternoon we were over the Continental Shelf and into the ocean proper. Ahead was Newfoundland, over one and a half thousand miles away across the North Atlantic. I thought of the boats who would already be well on their way south, following the warm and relatively kind Azores route, and remembered my voyage along the same route three years before. The passage had been remarkable for the fact that I had been terrified for the first thousand miles and scared for the next two and a half. It hadn't been a very enjoyable trip. But, although I was now facing a much less hospitable piece of ocean and should have been much more nervous than before, I didn't feel so.

For one thing I had sailed 15,000 miles since the first trip and that would blunt the edge of anyone's nervousness, and for another, I knew the *Golly* well enough to trust her in almost any conditions. Furthermore I did not plan to let my imagination have very much thinking time, unlike my previous trip when I had seen giant squids in every wave. Being unnecessarily worried is very wearing and I was determined not to get frightened unless absolutely necessary. This meant looking no further than a few miles and one weather forecast ahead. As a first step I marked the Quarter-Way Stage on the chart. This was my first destination, just 700 miles away, and just about all I could contemplate with equanimity.

What did worry me was a nasty familiar feeling in the pit of my stomach that was closely followed by a necessarily rapid sprint to the head. I groaned in dismay. Unless I was very much mistaken, it was the dreaded Lurgy again.

5

I hadn't been eating well since leaving Plymouth, but then I never did for the first few days of a sea passage. But as I made yet another run for the head, I reflected that this lack of food wasn't important now; whatever I ate traveled through so fast it couldn't do much good anyway. There was no doubt it was the Lurgy again. I had suffered the same diarrhea and lack of appetite twice before, once on my previous Atlantic crossing and again on a trip from Newport to Bermuda, and I remembered it only too well. I tried to think what made these voyages different from the many others I had made. On the Atlantic trip I had been alone and on the Bermuda voyage I and my companions had weathered a bad gale in the Gulf Stream, so it could easily have been fright that caused the problem. Certainly the symptoms were right. But, even when I tried, I couldn't feel truly frightened now, and I was certain it was something else.

As I changed sail at two in the morning, humping one large sail on deck and fighting the other down, then pulling the new sail up and hurrying back to winch it in, I flopped down exhausted in the cockpit and it suddenly came to me. The three voyages had one obvious thing in common. In every case I had suddenly started exerting an enormous amount of energy without getting much sleep. And, I was forced to admit, without having finished that extensive winter training program, my poor stomach muscles must be like piano strings. Every hour or so they were asked to perform feats of sail humping, hoisting, and winching in and then, just as they were thinking about relaxing over a good night's sleep, up they would be got and the whole thing would start again. It was really no wonder that they had got overactive in all the wrong directions. I thought of all that All Bran and gave a hollow laugh.

Even if I was losing weight by the hour, the boat was making marvelous progress by the minute. We roared along on a beam reach and managed 175 miles on our next day's run, the best that the *Golly* and I ever achieved together. With all those miles to our credit, we should reach the magical Quarter-Way Stage by the fifth or sixth day at sea. Then I would allow myself to look forward to the Third-of-the-Way Stage, and start thinking in terms of "Only twice as long again and I'll be there." This would seem almost nothing, with a bit of imagination, and soon after would come the Halfway Stage, the best of all.

I dragged my thoughts back to the Quarter-Way Stage. I was looking too far ahead again; any number of things could happen to slow us down, and I really must take each day as it came. But, as my eye slipped back across the chart to look at the halfway mark, I couldn't help planning my celebration dinner . . . a large plate of spaghetti, sweet chestnuts in cream . . .

It was no good dreaming of food if I couldn't force it down and I brought my mind back to the more immediate problem of the chores. That morning I was somewhat surprised to find that, for once, the washing up was not staring me in the eye as I stepped into the cockpit. This made a nice change, but at the same time I knew it was somewhere about and, despite the washing motion of the boat, would need attention. Then I remembered that I had wedged the bucket on the side deck to stop it sliding about and went to look for it there. But the side deck was quite empty and, suppressing my delight at the discovery, I tried to feel suitably cross with myself for losing a perfectly good bucket overboard with all that fine china and cutlery in it.

The washing-up problem solved for the day, I carried out my daily inspection of the self-steering to find that, as usual, a shackle needed replacing or a line tightening. I also examined the radio regularly to make sure it was not being dripped upon or otherwise mistreated. It was working beautifully and I was getting through to Portishead and Jack Hill without any trouble at all, but now for the first time there was heavy spray coming over the deck and I watched the point above the radio with anxiety. Sure enough, as if in response to my glare, a drip appeared, shortly followed by another. I wasn't going to take any chances and stuck a polyethylene sheet to the bulkhead and over the radio at an angle that would deflect the water onto the floor or my bunk, whichever was downhill. Normally water was strictly forbidden to come anywhere near my bunk, but anything was preferable to the isolation I would feel if I couldn't talk over that marvelous radio.

As I reminded myself frequently, all my problems were small. I was confident my stomach would unknot itself soon and in the meantime it was doing wonderful things for my figure. Even though I rarely slept for more than an hour at a stretch, I was not feeling unpleasantly tired, just nicely weary. This had the effect of dulling my thinking — no bad thing when alone and miles from anywhere, for it is best not to think about such grand things as large oceans and small boats in case it makes one unnecessarily nervous; nor is it wise to think about loving families too often. I felt pangs of loneliness from time to time anyway and I had no wish to experience more; weariness was making me emotional and, unless I took care, thoughts of the people and things I missed brought on damp eyes and a trembling lower lip.

Most of the time I kept myself too busy to think. By the time I had done all the chores, kept the boat sailing, and slept, there wasn't much time for anything else.

Of course I knew the following winds and fast sailing were too good to last, so when the wind started to veer around to the southwest I was not too surprised. Soon it would be wet, windy, and unpleasant, just like it always was in the Atlantic. Just got to get used to it, I thought as I shuffled around the wet foredeck struggling with a flogging sail. And after all what was a boot full of water as long as the rest of me was dry? I drained the boot, removed a ghastly sock, and gave my toes a violent rubbing to thaw them out. Doubtless this was to be the pattern of life to come, but just to be sure I decided to listen to the weather forecast, something I rarely enjoyed hearing but couldn't bear to miss. However on this occasion I would have to be content to miss it; as usual I had switched on five minutes too late.

At two in the morning on June 9, a nasty suspicion began to enter my mind. The barometer had dropped, and the wind was freshening all the time. The night had become very black, and although I could not see the sky, I knew it would be covered with gray scudding clouds. I do not like to believe the worst unless absolutely necessary, but the weather seemed to have all the makings of a gale and I prepared accordingly. I made sure everything was well stowed and securely fastened, I put on plenty of warm clothes under my most waterproof oilskins and I put some face cream and absorbent cotton in a strategic position. The cream was essential if my face was not to emerge as a salt-encrusted relic, while the cotton was the best possible material for earplugs, very necessary to reduce some of the appalling din that a gale produces. Then I settled down to wait, dozing as best I could.

There cannot be many worse awakenings than the one I had that morning. As the gloomy half-light of dawn filtered into the cabin, I heard the wind shriek in the rigging and the thunderous crash of the bows sinking into large waves. Water poured over the decks and down the ports and there was the ominous sound of water slapping up from full bilges. The *Golly* was heeled well over and I could almost feel her struggling under the excess of sail. It was time for me to get up. People wonder how one can find the willpower to leave a warm sleeping bag and get up after only a short sleep, but when the weather is worsening it's no problem at all. After changing down to the storm jib and putting the third and last reef in the main I sat in the shelter of the cockpit's sprayhood to watch over the boat. The wind was now blasting across the sea and the waves were gray with long white streaks blown from their crests. It was blowing a gale and from the west so that, much as she struggled, the *Golly* could hardly make any worthwhile progress. Her course was northwesterly but, allowing for considerable leeway, her track must be almost northerly. It was not a direction in which I wanted to go. We were already farther north than I had intended and I was uneasy at the thought of being pushed even farther off course, for it would be difficult to claw back toward the south against the prevailing winds.

As the gale continued to blow, the seas built up and the *Golly* crashed and shuddered into the waves until the din was awful. More and more water poured over the decks and soon everything was dripping with moisture and imbued with damp. Finally, when a particularly powerful gust blasted down on us I could bear it no longer and, crawling carefully along the deck, I lowered the jib and then the mainsail to provide some much-needed peace. The *Golly* was quite happy without any sail up and lay beam on to the seas, rising to each wave until the crest had passed noisily away beneath. Inside the boat, the worst of the din had ceased, and the motion was almost gentle. Of course we were being blown back the way we had come, but at that moment I didn't mind very much; I could only think how delightfully peaceful it was compared to pushing on into those seas. I might even be able to get some sleep.

Before going below I noticed that the main halyard had snagged itself around a permanently mounted radar reflector on the front of the mast. This reflector was cylindrical and perfectly smooth and theoretically unable to snag anything, but the halyard was firmly and obstinately looped around it. I clambered carefully along the rolling deck and fastened myself like a limpet to the mast where I pulled and flicked and jerked the halyard until I could think of no new combination of flicks and jerks that might unravel it. Finally, after half an hour's tussle, I knew I was beaten and, before I dropped with the effort, I decided to give in gracefully and try again later. I made up the end of the halyard and gave a last look at the troublesome reflector just in time to see the mast whip forward and the halyard free itself.

It was an endlessly unpleasant day. Despite earplugs like corks, I could not sleep, always preferring to return to the cockpit to watch the cheerless scene. I sat there in a mesmerized state of misery, feeling my clothes damp and clammy against my skin and shivering as each gust seemed to blow straight through my oilskins. At one point the wind decreased a little and I galvanized myself into action, crawling slowly along the deck and rehoisting the storm jib and reefed main. It was nice to be making progress again, however small, but I still wasn't sure it was worth the crashing and shuddering as the *Golly* corkscrewed up a wave and leaped over the top. Every quarter of an hour I pumped the bilge, but otherwise I remained in the cockpit, nibbling on oatcakes, which were the only food I could get down. My visits to the head had become less frequent but were still necessary every hour or so and I dreaded them, for the action of the boat made the head compartment an uncomfortable, not to say perilous place, where it was necessary to cling steadfastly to prevent a dreadful accident from occurring.

Back in the cockpit I dozed from time to time and as soon as my eyes closed that lovely and endlessly desirable vision would leap into my mind. A person, usually Jacques, would appear in the main hatchway looking calm, rested, and terribly competent. He would smile, beckon, and say, "Come down now and sleep. I'll look after everything." And I couldn't be sure, but I thought there may have been the beautiful aroma of hot soup floating up from the galley. Then I would awake with a jerk and try to adjust to the cold knowledge that I was alone, very damp, and terribly miserable. I succeeded many times, but there were other times when I didn't, and I would shake my head, moan and mutter about "absolutely finally never again" and "absolutely nuts" and "I don't *have* to be here!" and then I'd remember that I *was here* unless I could spirit myself to land by sheer willpower. Sometimes I had wild thoughts about how nice it would be if the boat sank and I popped into the life raft to be rescued by a ship with an enormously hot bath, a large warm bed, and endless hot meals. But more often than not I thought of my family and of people in general and how marvelous they all were and had a small cry, after which everything seemed very much better and I wondered what I had been unhappy about in the first place.

I decided I must really cheer myself up, but at first I was a bit stuck as to how I could do it. I couldn't phone Jacques because he was at work. And I couldn't get any food down, although the cook was on strike anyway and I wouldn't have got anything hot. But I could change into some dry clothes, and I did. The lockers themselves were wet from bilge water that had shot all the way up the sides of the boat when she lurched, but the clothes in their plastic bags were dry and, after stripping off my damp and sticky layers (the paper panties were easy, they fell apart in my hands), I was soon warm as toast. By two in the morning, 24 hours after it had started, the gale finally moderated and, full of zest, I sprang up onto the foredeck to put up more sail. Five minutes later an arm, a leg, and most of my bottom were soaked. For the first time I said a very rude word.

Although I had the enthusiasm to change sail, I was surprised to find how difficult it had become. It took much more time and effort to move the heavy sails around and the hoisting and winching nearly exhausted me so that I lay recovering in the cockpit for a long time after. Clearly I had to eat more and I started by forcing down an enormous meal of dry bread, several spoons of honey, a tin of peaches, and the last of the fresh milk. Ignoring my damp clothes, I fell into my sleeping bag and, apart from an occasional look up through the hatch, I slept for a long and uninterrupted four hours.

The *Golly* and I had weathered our first gale and, overlooking all the wet and misery, it had not been too bad. The important thing was that nothing had broken or fallen off or come loose, apart from the ship's mascot, the little golly, who had thrown himself across the cabin in disgust.

Now came the long task of cleaning up and I started by tidying up my bunk and having another short rest, just to summon up some strength. After an hour I decided I would definitely get up in ten minutes, and reached for a book. It was a surprisingly interesting book and I was amazed to discover that I had read three chapters in just under an hour. Then I felt tired again and, it being important to catch up on sleep, I thought I'd better have a quick nap. The morning passed in no time and I barely had a moment to hang up some damp clothes and to find out that the heater didn't work before it was time to call Jack Hill and give him my news. It was marvelous to talk to Jack; he always cheered me up and boosted my morale as well as giving me welcome news, both of my family and of other competitors.

The news of the other competitors was mixed. There had already been some retirements, but nothing was known about the many boats without transmitters. Those who could report their positions already seemed to be well spread out. Jack was sure I was doing well, but even if I could be certain he was right it meant little at this stage; there was still a long way to go. Jack kept asking how I was and I finally told him I wasn't feeling too well. "Well we won't mention too much about that," he said, "it might worry your family." It was typical of Jack's thoughtfulness.

Life in the freezing cold of the Grand Banks was going to be miserable without a heater, so, feeling at my most efficient, I tackled it as soon as I had finished my call to Jack. The tiny nozzle that sprayed the pressurized fuel out of the tank into the fuel line had become blocked. Thinking how brilliant I was, I stuck a sewing needle into the tiny hole and wiggled it around, whereupon the tip promptly broke and sealed the nozzle as firmly as a cork. After that success I turned my attention to filming, a chore I liked even less as time went on. I shot two rolls in a manner worthy of Cecil B. De Mille then played back the tape to check the sound. My voice was there, but it was hardly discernible beneath a high-pitched whine. I examined the tape recorder and thought the trouble might have something to do with the water that trickled out of its casing. If it was going to be that kind of day, I didn't think it was worth tackling more jobs and retired to my bunk for a snooze, remaining there for the rest of the afternoon.

Although I managed to get through to Jack Hill without much difficulty during the day, I discovered that it was not so easy to make radio-telephone calls at night, not for any technical reasons but because the entire merchant navy seemed to be calling their wives. The procedure was to wait until a conversation was finished then to speak to the operator and ask to be given a place in the line of ships waiting to make calls. On a busy evening there might be five or six ships ahead in the line and, to be sure I did not miss my turn, I had to leave the radio on and keep an ear open for my call sign. At first I was appalled at the idea of having to listen to a series of private telephone conversations, but then I realized that everyone who used the service was well aware that the calls were, in fact, public and adjusted their conversations accordingly so that their dialogue was rich with nuance and innuendo. That evening there was one conversation I found very difficult not to hear.

"How's that present I gave you?"

"What present?"

"You know! *That* present . . . the one I gave you." There was a long pause.

"Oh . . . you mean . . . not the . . . the brooch from last Christmas?"

"No, no!" said the other impatiently. "The special *thing* I gave you to . . . to . . . to . . . to remember me by! *You* know."

But at last it was my turn and within minutes I was talking to Jacques at the farm. "Did you have a miserable time, love?" he asked anxiously. I didn't want to worry him unnecessarily but said yes anyway because I was still feeling rather damp and fed up. Sympathy must have been just what I needed because, having recounted every drenching and bruising received, I felt immeasurably better. In the next ten minutes we managed to cover the height of the broad beans, a full description of my menu, and the state of Jacques's visa application. Finally his eminently practical mind came up with a brilliant idea for unblocking the heater nozzle by approaching it from the other side, and we said good-bye.

The next day I reached the Quarter-Way Stage still one day ahead of my target. Despite the gale I had sailed 700 miles in six days, and celebrated by feeling hungry for almost the first time since leaving Plymouth. At last the wind was abaft the beam and the boat upright and I was able to cook and do other chores without the enormous difficulties I encountered when the boat was heeled over. I chose a dried prawn curry for my special feast but only ate half of it. Either I had read the instruction wrong or it tasted like half-hydrated prawn curry. But I quickly overcame this disappointment with a whole tin of plums mixed with some custard, which was delicious. It looked as though I was developing a passion for plums, which was just as well because I still had another 25 large tins to get through.

As a Quarter-Way present, I allowed myself to look at the mysterious parcels that Jacques had given me and discovered that he had correctly anticipated my requirements for mental stimulation by putting in metal puzzles for 12-year-olds and children's Plasticine.

My celebration day wouldn't be complete without getting the heater to work, because unless I could dry out some clothes, I would be in for a very damp few weeks. As Jacques had suggested, I approached the blocked nozzle from the other side and the needle tip immediately shot out followed quickly by the original criminal, a bit of grit. My morale now high, I lit the stove and sat back to watch the steam rising from my long johns. But to my surprise I noticed that steam or rather smoke was appearing from the heater instead. I put my head underneath the heater to investigate and, as a blast of kerosene fumes covered my face, I realized the problem. The wind, though not very strong, was causing a downdraft in the flue. Congratulating myself on my brilliance, I went up on deck and blocked off most of the flue by pressing aluminum foil around the cowl. In this way I twice managed to fill the boat with fumes, but finally, after much trial and error, I seemed to get it right and was able to watch my clothes drying board hard and white with salt.

It had been a very successful day and I felt very cheerful as long as I ignored the weather. The wind was nudging back toward the southwest again and increasing. It had all the looks of another wet interlude and by afternoon it was; I struggled on the foredeck to raise the working jib and take another reef in the main. I resigned myself to another blow but was delighted to find the wind suddenly backed and moderated. This was a nice surprise and I contemplated putting up more sail, but didn't rush into it because a sail change on the *Golly* still laid me out for half an hour. But the wind kept dropping and eventually I had to put up a larger jib or watch the *Golly* wallow in the swell.

No sooner was the sail up and pulling than the wind changed direction and increased again, so that once again I had too much sail up. Bother it, I thought, I'll leave it up and never mind. Immediately, a large black cloud came along with a squall underneath it and I was forced to shorten sail or have the boat sitting on her side. After another half hour the cloud passed and the wind dropped again. I could see it was going to be one of those nights. A weather forecast would be useful, but now that I was out of range of Radio 2 and the BBC shipping forecasts, it would have to come from elsewhere. Just before the start we had all been handed a brochure on the BBC Overseas Service together with a note saying that a special race forecast would be transmitted at 0330 GMT every day. This was ideal and I looked for the required frequency on the Brookes and Gatehouse receiver. After a few minutes and with a great feeling of disappointment, I decided I didn't have it. Of course it was staring me in the face but, with my brain in slow gear, I kept looking at the wrong set of radio bands.

No forecast could have told me that the wind would twist and turn, blow and then moderate throughout the night. At three in the morning I found myself lying panting in the cockpit having just changed down yet again, only to find the wind moderating once more. There is good seamanship and ridiculous keenness; I decided it was good seamanship to leave her undercanvased and ridiculous keenness to put up more sail again. I didn't have the strength to be keen anyway, and I staggered below to rest my shaking limbs. Soon I was able to congratulate myself on my foresight because another rain squall hit the boat and she was no longer undercanvased. After an hour's dozing I thought that I had really been very clever, because the squall was still blowing. About an hour later it began to occur to me that this was the longest squall I had ever experienced and, despite a very strong desire to roll over, block my ears, and go to sleep, I pulled myself up and had a look outside. By that time the gale was well established and I found the *Golly* to be overpowered yet again. With a mental groan I staggered up on deck to pull down the flapping jib, to receive the compulsory shot of water down the neck, and to get another smaller jib onto the forestay. As soon as I had winched the sail in, a strong blast of wind hit my cheek and I noticed with interest that the anemometer read well over 40 knots of wind. Another blast and I went back on deck to lower everything, managing, yet again, to wrap the main halyard around the radar reflector. This time I wasn't going to waste all that effort by trying to free it and I waited patiently for the action of the mast to whip it clear. No good watching it; of course, it would never free itself so I slipped back to the cockpit and looked the other way. After several secretive glances I gave up the subtle approach and charged at the halyard, preparing myself to flick and jerk at it for hours. I gave a first almighty heave, prepared for a massive jerk, and looked up to see the halyard swinging free as a bird.

The gale finally settled in from the south and it was possible to make slow progress west under storm jib and treble reefed main. But if the first gale was unpleasant, this one on the seventh day was appalling. Not only was I feeling unprepared for another blow so soon after the first, but I was already exhausted from the sail changing throughout the night. And, needless to add, I was soaking wet. But at least I could do something about my wet clothes and, full of anticipation, I went below to search out some dry ones. It was an impossible job. Every time I put my hand into a locker it came out wet, and as I discovered more and more dripping garments, my heart sank farther and farther. I could put up with a lot of discomfort for a short time, but the prospect of being wet for another three weeks was almost impossible to imagine. Out of piles of wet jeans, soaking sweaters, and clammy socks I salvaged one suit of polar underwear and a jersey. These I carefully hung on the clothesline over the stove where I defied a tidal wave to reach them. From my position in the bunk, I watched over them with loving care. One day when all the world was dry, I would put on those wonderful clothes.

The lockers had become wet from the bilge water that was being flung up the sides of the boat as the *Golly* jerked and gyrated over the waves. But the bilge itself was being filled with water from the toerail, the mast, and various leaks of uncertain origin in the deck. The toerail had soaked nearly all my books and had wet most of the food stowed in the galley. Half my store of bread had got damp and I could almost see the mildew growing before my eyes. All the towels were dripping and I didn't dare look in the locker where the toilet paper was kept. The leak above the radio was in full flood, but I managed to catch a lot of it by balancing a cooking pot in a strategic position underneath. All I had to do was to remember to empty it every 15 minutes before it got too full and the contents were shot across the cabin by a sudden movement of the boat.

The movements of the boat were severe. She would rush at a wave, leap off the top, and then crash down onto the other side, give a quick roll or flip, then rush at another. Sometimes she found nothing but air as she leaped off a crest and there would be a ghastly moment of silence before a terrible shuddering crash as the bows hit water again. At times like that it was easy to imagine that the mast had just broken or the hull split in two, for it seemed impossible that any boat could take such a beating. But with the *Golly* it was all or nothing and I could not slow her down without stopping her altogether. So I left her as she was, water streaming over the decks (and into the lockers) and her motion as wild as a washing machine's. Like a dirty dishcloth I was spun, rinsed, and tumbled about until I should have been whiter than white. I tried wedging myself in my bunk but nearly got thrown out, so I tied myself in and lay there in a state of mental paralysis, allowing no thoughts to enter my mind. I heard a banging and crashing sound above the racket of the gale but was too tired to go and investigate, choosing to watch the water spurting out from beside the mast instead. Even if I had known the toilet had broken loose and was committing hara-kiri by painful degrees I wouldn't have minded much — my memories of it were not exactly pleasant. But then another noise came to my bleary attention and this one could not be ignored. Something was hitting against the hull and even before I looked I knew what it would be. I had tied a sail down along the deck and, sure enough, the weight of water had pulled it free so that most of it was trailing in the sea. Five minutes later I had the sail below and another boot full of water. If life was bleak then it was even more bleak three hours later. I allowed myself to become excited at the sight of a clear sky ahead and, quite certain the wind would drop, waited expectantly. The sun came out, the clouds disappeared, and then, to my dismay, the wind blew as strongly as ever, if not stronger.

So this was the great adventure, I thought disconsolately. Gales that went on forever, wet long johns, soggy food that was impossible to cook, damp books that fell apart in your hands, and above all, no one to complain to. Of course there was a bright side. The *Golly* was managing herself very well and was giving me no cause for concern. Also lit by the bright sunshine, the windswept sea did look magnificent as the great waves rolled across it in endless procession. It was just a pity we had to soldier through them. And there was the knowledge that the gale had to end sometime, although as the hours went by I couldn't help feeling a nagging doubt.

Once the gale would be over, life would improve. There had to be some gentle breezes and calm seas ahead. Then I would be able to sleep again, and eat again and, above all, be dry again — although I had some doubts about that too.

6

Gales go on forever and then miraculously they end. At three the next morning the wind had dropped enough for me to put up more sail, breathe a sigh of relief and, together with my hot-water bottle, snuggle up in a bunk and get some sleep.

The next morning I woke up feeling as though I had just come through a bout with Muhammad Ali. I was covered with bruises, woolly in the head, and stiff all over. Changing sail seemed to take even longer than usual and I felt as weak as a kitten. "Must eat," I declared and made myself some porridge, which was no mean feat because the *Golly* was still at an impossible angle. Strangely, the wind had not died away or veered as it usually did after a gale. Instead it was a steady Force 5 or 6 from the west and the boat was hard on the wind, pushing through a lumpy sea.

I didn't even begin to think what the weather might be planning and concentrated on getting some porridge down instead. I managed half of it, which was quite good, but I wished I could eat more. My weakness seemed to be worse and after the slightest exertion I had to sit down and rest.

Mother would have been horrified and I only wished she were here with me to cook something for which I had an appetite.

At least my visits to the head were less frequent although, as I discovered, there wasn't much head left to visit. The seat and cover had torn themselves off and smashed to pieces. On an ordinary marine toilet this wouldn't matter, but the Lavac relied on the seat and cover forming a perfect seal so that the pressure in the bowl could be dropped by pumping. No seat and cover — no head. Luckily I still had one plastic bucket left and this became my head under the stars, very much easier to use and the scenery was a great improvement.

Sunday was one of my days for calling Jack Hill, but it was also the day when Jacques would be there at Lymington and I looked forward to making the call with special excitement. When I got through I found there were more people there than I had bargained for. Bob Saunders and the BBC were by the phone anxious to know how my filming was going and whether the equipment was working well. It was difficult to know how to express my feelings about the filming over a public radio-telephone service and I restricted my remarks to problems like the tape recorder's scream and the camera that kept falling apart in my hands and the switches that wouldn't switch. Bob Saunders told me I was doing a great job and that I was marvelous and a few other nice things, and I thought that perhaps I wouldn't strangle him on arrival at Newport, just condemn him to three months filming himself with his own equipment, preferably while rowing the Amazon singlehanded.

But it was marvelous to talk to the two J's and after telling them I was wet, miserable, but perfectly all right, they gave me news of the race. Twelve boats had retired and I was very glad to hear that Dominique Berthier, one of the French girls, had been safely picked up from her life raft after her boat had sunk in collision with a ship.

Jacques also told me where to find the frequency for the weather forecasts on the Brookes and Gatehouse receiver, and as soon as he told me, I realized how stupid I'd been. (I'd been looking on all the shortwave bands but not on the marine band, thinking the BBC never used it for World Service transmissions.)

In turn I was able to report that, after eight days at sea, I was expecting to have sailed 900 miles by noon that day, very nearly one third of the way, and this despite two gales. I felt it was a great achievement for the *Golly* and me, and told them I was very pleased. But I carefully did not mention that I was still feeling weak; I could not bear the thought of worrying everyone. Anyway, I was certain I would be feeling better soon. Instead I assured Jacques that I was eating like a horse, and because he didn't believe a word of it, I described the enormous and luscious breakfast I was supposed to have had that morning, complete with sound effects and rumbles of contentment. He still didn't believe a word and let me off with a stern warning to eat or else.

I felt immeasurably more cheerful after the call and set to work on the chores with something like enthusiasm. While I was sitting in the cockpit thinking about doing the washing up, some dolphins came along to play and I stopped work to watch them leaping and diving around the bows, their whistling signals clearly audible as they chatted among themselves. We had been asked to report all sightings of dolphins and whales, so I looked at them carefully to be sure I described their markings correctly. But the ones around the bows were moving too quickly and I moved aft to where another group were swimming more sedately. I peered at them, and suddenly felt a prickly sensation down my spine. They weren't dolphins at all, they were small whales. After the number of yachts sunk by killer whales in recent years, I hurried below to get the reference book and flicked through the soggy pages with fumbling haste. But with relief I was able to rule out killer whales or, the worst of all, baby killer whales with angry mothers in hot pursuit. No, these appeared to be pilot whales, which were very harmless and, apparently, not too bright because they followed their leader anywhere, even up beaches. I was very flattered that they had chosen to follow me but hoped they would find their leader soon.

I think I may have found him first. Two hours later I was on the bows watching dolphins again when I saw a whale right in the boat's path. I had the unpleasant feeling he was having a nap and I hardly knew whether to rush back to the tiller where I would undoubtedly arrive too late to avoid him or to yell something like "Wake up, mate!" So I stood there frozen with indecision. Luckily he had his radar plugged in and very gently and certainly not in any particular hurry, he sank beneath the surface just as the *Golly's* bows rushed over him. I waited for a bump as he met the keel, hoping he was not in the mood for a lovely back scratch, but I felt nothing and breathed again.

The wind went around to the south that afternoon and the visibility dropped until I thought it wise to put up another radar reflector for the benefit of ships. Not that I had seen a single one. The North Atlantic was meant to be a busy place, but no ships seemed to come up here and what with the weather and the visibility, I could see why. I looked for ships at least once an hour through the day and night, and usually more often, but I had seen nothing since the Scillies. And it was not as if I missed them in bad visibility, for I had a marvelous little gadget that gave me eyes. Radar itself was banned in the race, but there was nothing to prevent me carrying a radar detector. This little box picked up the radar signals of ships and "pinged" at each sweep of their scanners. But more important, if there were no ships about, it didn't ping at all — assuming ships had their radar on, of course, and if they didn't in this visibility, I was in trouble. So silence from the little black box meant I was safe for at least half an hour and could go below and sleep with some degree of confidence. It was no good in clear weather, because few ships kept their radar on when they could see, but now as the mist rolled in across the ocean it was a great reassurance.

The wind was worrying me. It was now coming from the

south at a steady Force 6, just as it had before the last gale, and I had a nasty feeling in the pit of my stomach, a surprisingly accurate omen of bad weather. And my stomach wasn't the only thing with that sinking feeling; I looked at the barometer and saw that it had taken a nasty plunge. Well, at least I would have a weather forecast to listen to that night, and doubtless it would not be as bad as it looked.

In the meantime I remembered Jacques's warnings and made myself a good meal and, what was more, I actually ate it. I started with a pizza, which resembled cheese-flavored leather, ate the last few unwilted lettuce leaves with some tomatoes, and finished with plums and custard. I felt so full I had to lie down and recover.

To complete a good day, I called my parents. I had been planning to phone them for several days, but somehow a gale had always intervened. I waited at the end of a long line of merchant seamen anxious to speak to their wives. It was obviously going to be a long time before I was connected, so I turned the transmitter and the engine off, leaving only the receiver on to save power and fuel. But I had not allowed for the marvelous operators at Portishead. At the end of the next conversation and a long way ahead of my turn, I suddenly heard my call sign and, after a panic to get the transmitter on and warmed up again, I was through. It was only one instance of the many kind favors they did me.

"Are you eating and keeping warm and taking care and feeling all right?" asked Mother in one breath.

"And clipping on your safety harness?" added Father.

I said yes, of course, absolutely no need to worry, and the thermonuclear underwear was doing a great job. After which we turned to mundane matters like dates of arrival and flights and telephone numbers and how one got a toilet seat through the U.S. Customs. "But," asked Father, "most important of all, are you getting the forecasts all right? There's one I got from Arthur Blackham today that shows . . ."

I interrupted Father and pointed out that, much as I would love the forecast, I was not allowed to receive special weather information and would have to wait for the BBC broadcast that night.

"Well . . . yes . . . but do take special care, won't you!" said Father enigmatically. And I wondered why he sounded so worried.

That night, at 0330 GMT, I tuned into the BBC Overseas Service for the special weather forecast. I picked up the broadcast very well indeed; I clearly heard the man say "Southwest wind gale Force 7 to 9, increasing storm Force 10 later." Well, that's useful, I thought, I must listen to that forecast every night. And with that I turned in for some sleep. There would be plenty of time to do everything that had to be done in the morning and in the meantime I was going to escape to the land of nod, where dreamboats were manned by crews of 12, and never went to sea in anything more than Force 2.

There was an old familiar feeling about the wet, dripping boat, the sound of the wind shrieking in the rigging, and the sensation of a boot full of water. I was beginning to feel as though I had been thrown about, blown at, and sprayed on all my life, and I puttered happily about the boat, doing this and that, as if it were all quite normal. And, after the last week's weather, it almost was.

I even managed to do some filming, which was an effort I was justifiably proud of, for it entailed fixing a camera onto a bracket on the stern, a place where the motion of the boat resembled a roller coaster. While on the stern I also checked the self-steering, a constant source of anxiety in bad weather, for it slammed badly from side to side and I feared that the main casting might become damaged. I tightened the preventer lines to stop the gear swinging too far and decided to inspect it at least once every hour.

At midday some sort of front passed over, for the clouds cleared away and the sun came out. But this time I wasn't fooled and expected no improvement in the weather. It was just as well, for the wind suddenly screamed in the rigging

My first attempt at helming,
at the age of seven

A last coat of anti-fouling
before the start

inter training

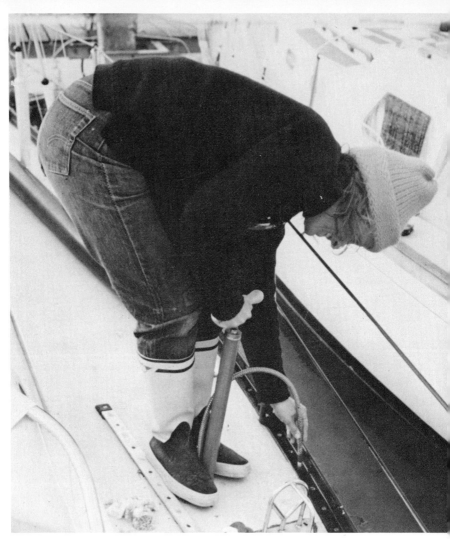

Finding the leaks in the toerail—
with the aid of a bicycle pump

Sitting in the *Golly's* coc'
wondering if I could e
handle

Holding on by my toes
to fix the self-steering—
a taste of things to come

A final "good luck" toast
from my parents

With Jacques, taking a break
from the eternal preparations

Smooth down-wind sailing
and a good view of the *Golly's* troublesome
self-steering gear

Hoisting a sail
on one of the
powerful winches

A calm sea, a pulling spinnaker,
and a good sextant sight—
all the best and none
of the worst of sailing

Trying to lower
the genoa without
dropping it in the water

Gale force conditions and the *Golly*
heels to a breaking wave

My impeccable repair
work on the self-steering!

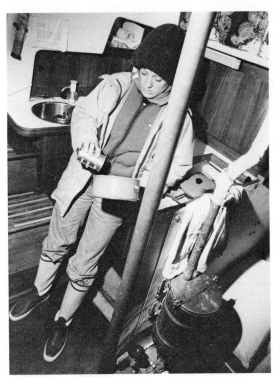

Cooking at
an angle was
never easy

Using the radio—
my life-line
throughout the race

Pidge trying to balance
on the guardwire

A shaky photograph of
the icebergs, now safely behind me

Feeling wet, cold,
and dejected

Checking the bank of instruments

Receiving the Ladies' Trophy
from Mrs. Mary Thomas (Photo:
Charles Parker)

and the *Golly* heeled. It was blowing a severe gale, Force 9, and I hurried to lower the tiny storm jib and treble reefed main. I then tidied up the deck as best I could, crawling around on hands and knees, and taking care to hold on tight. I wanted to leave nothing on deck that might pull free and be swept over the side. More blasts of wind hit the boat, crying and shrieking in the rigging. Head down, I crawled crab-fashion back to the cockpit where I noticed that the wind speed indicator was reading over 50 knots and sometimes 55, which put it at storm Force 10. I kept thinking that I should be feeling more worried and wondered why I wasn't. Doubtless it was the familiarity of the scene; across the sea marched an endless procession of large rolling waves covered in spindrift and breaking crests. But as the hours passed the waves became much larger than I had ever seen before. Sitting in their troughs was like lying in a great valley completely surrounded by mountains that blocked out the view. Then as a wave approached, the *Golly* would rise out of the trough and up the slope until, suddenly, she was at the top of the world and below her was spread a breathtaking scene of white peaks that stretched on forever.

If she could have stayed on top of those waves it would have been even more beautiful, but inevitably she would start to slip down again until she was sitting in the depths of the valley. There I would cast an anxious eye at the next crest to see if it was going to break before it reached us or not. Whenever I decided it was going to break on or over the boat I would brace myself, close my eyes, and wait for the crash as the roaring, breaking water thundered into the boat. The *Golly* lay ahull in her usual fashion, beam on the waves but sometimes a little stern to, sometimes a little bow to. When a breaking crest roared up she would heel over, let it crash into her side, and then shake off the water, ready for the next. I always braced myself for the wave that would roll her a little too far or drop her into a trough but it never came, for the *Golly* was a real old sea dog and never let herself be caught out. Several times waves filled the cockpit or shot over the boat but, apart from a sharp lurch or a small roll, the *Golly* remained unperturbed.

Later I read that the wave heights had been measured at 35 feet in my area and 40 feet in the center of the storm not far away — large by Atlantic standards and enormous by mine. But, oddly enough, these seas were not as uncomfortable or dangerous as some smaller seas I had met. They were well spaced with long slopes that enabled the *Golly* to bob over them whereas steeper, smaller seas can overwhelm a yacht, or throw her down into their troughs.

Soon it occurred to me that the *Golly* was looking after herself very well and that I would be much drier down below with the hatch closed. But it was a strange sensation to be shut in that dark cabin listening to the screeching and howling of that wind and the occasional roar of a breaking crest. I tried doing my usual imitation of an ostrich by sticking absorbent cotton in my ears and burying my head under the pillow, but I slept little. I was particularly worried about ships, for they would never see a small yacht in these seas. And I worried about the self-steering gear. Every time a wave pushed against the *Golly*, the pendulum section of the gear would be jerked violently sideways until it was brought up short by the preventers. But the strains were enormous and the preventers were vibrating with tension as they took the load. I watched them uneasily but could think of nothing that I could attach to take some of the strain off them.

After one short and fitful doze I slid back the hatch to have a quick look around and saw, with horror, that the very thing I feared had finally happened. The strain on the gear had proved too much and one of the preventer lines had pulled so hard that two of the support struts had buckled out of all recognition. On taking a closer look I also noticed that, without their support, the main casting was taking a terrible bashing. That had to be stopped and quickly, for if the main casting sheared that would be the end of the self-steering. Hastily I tightened the tiller lines to stop the gear swinging, then instantly regretted it. The bent struts buckled even further, just like putty.

What a mess I was making of everything. It might have been better to have a think before leaping into action. Hoping it wasn't too late now, I crouched under the sprayhood and urged my brain to do the necessary. At first it would only think about how one got back to England without self-steering and other such depressing things, and I had to force it to consider how I might stop that casting getting bashed. The solution was very simple of course, but it only took me forever to work out that I must wear the boat around onto the other tack so that the undamaged port struts could take the strain. Easy. Then, all I had to do was to straighten those struts. Not at all easy.

I got the *Golly* settled on the other tack and eyed the struts. Somewhere, it suddenly occurred to me, there was a spare strut, maybe even two! Next moment I was upside down in one locker, then the next, then the stern locker, desperately searching for those spares. From time to time water poured down my back or my arm, but I hardly noticed in my frenetic search. At last, in the darkest, deepest corner of the stern locker I found one, but try as I might I could find no other.

By this time I was in need of a morale boost as well as information and called Jacques at the farm. It was incredible that I could be speaking to him in the middle of a storm somewhere in the Atlantic and that he was there by the writing desk, looking out over the barn full of hay and the field beyond. Our conversation was necessarily short and to the point because I was having to shout above the noise of the wind and general clatter, but he soon confirmed that there was only the one spare strut, as I had feared. So I would have to straighten one of the bent ones and we agreed I should try a combination of heat, hammer, and whatever brute force I could muster. It was not a very happy me that said good-bye that evening, and Jacques must have felt miserably worried and helpless as he put the phone down.

Tied securely on to the backstay and the pushpit, I leaned as far as I could over the rail and started to remove the struts. The wind had moderated to a Force 8 to 9 gale, although I would never have known the difference from my position over the stern. One moment the sea was far below me and the next it was rushing up toward me and the water was lapping around my armpits. I closed my eyes and concentrated on holding onto the two wrenches in my hands and about five nuts and bolts between my teeth. I only hoped I didn't swallow. After 20 minutes I had removed both the bent struts with the loss of only one washer, an achievement of which I was very proud. After crawling back into the cabin I had a short rest, grabbed some oatcakes, which had constituted my total diet for the previous two days, and set to work. Welding was not one of the arts they had taught me at the young ladies' establishment I attended, nor did they get around to metal forging or ironwork. But I'll try anything once if I have to, and on this occasion I'd have tried anything 50 times.

For the next four hours the boat reverberated to hammer strokes, grunts, wheezes, and the sound of sizzling metal. I heated that strut, I hit it, I pulled on it, I wrenched it, I put it in a vise and sat on it, I wedged it between two pieces of strong wood and jumped on it. Sometimes I just looked at it and asked it. Finally, as I sat in a collapsed bundle unable to do more, I regarded the results of my labors. The strut was a lot less bent than before. At the same time it was not exactly straight. There were a number of kinks and curves that I could not seem to get out. But it was the best I could do, and unable to face an hour upside down over the stern in the darkness, I turned in for some sleep, noting in my log the sage comment: "Lord, what a climate."

Dawn is not my favorite time and I can think of better ways of spending it than threading nuts onto bolts underwater by feel. But I had already lost eight hours progress during the night and was anxious to find out whether the strut would hold, in which case I could go on, or whether it would buckle again, in which case I would have to make slow and painful progress back to England. I spent an hour upside down over the stern of the *Golly*, putting the parts carefully into place, transferring nuts and bolts from my oilskin trousers to my teeth, and then fitting everything together with infinite care.

But at last it was done and without the loss of a single valuable part, which was a miracle. As I made a final check of the connections I looked over the rest of the gear before putting it to the test. At first I missed it, but the second time I saw it: a tiny hairline crack halfway across the main casting. This was grim indeed. But if I took care not to let it get bashed again and if there were no more gales it might just hold. . . .

Under storm jib and treble reefed main the *Golly* plodded slowly off into the last of the gale, while I watched the self-steering like a hawk. Many times I imagined that the strut was bending, but it was only tiredness playing tricks with my eyes. Finally I gave up keeping watch and crawled below to rest.

The exhaustion I felt was total. My wrestling with the strut had drained my energy and the storm had emptied my mind. I lay on my bunk in a heap, not bothering to remove my oilskins, just staring at the water spurting out from the mast above me. I was too tired to sleep and too cold to have the energy to get warm. I should have made an effort to do something, but apart from stuffing a soggy oatcake into my mouth, I couldn't be bothered. Finally, after much concentration, I did manage to close my eyes and then to sleep, only to have my rest colored by vivid dreams of ironworkers bending metal bars as if they were putty.

Much later that morning I pulled myself up and knew exactly what I must do. Before anything else, before I did the navigation, or changed another sail, before I ate another oatcake or plum, I must wash my hair — or, as I had christened it, my "spikes." My spikes stood up like the prickles on a hedgehog. Held in place by salt, and fashioned by the wind and my hats, they defied the hairbrush and itched like crazy.

Wedged against the sink, kettle of water in hand and shampoo close by, I washed my spikes until they became hair again. The feeling of relief was superb. I felt like a new person. Of course I hadn't actually washed the rest of me so I wouldn't have passed inspection. But I felt I could tackle anything, and that included a good wash on the next day, of course.

The wind was moderating all the time, and with something approaching energy, I jumped on deck to put up more sail. I checked and tightened the preventer lines on the self-steering. I made myself a late breakfast of porridge, fruit, and bread and marmalade, most of which I ate. And I called Jack Hill on the radio. He told me that there had been 17 retirements so far, of which no less than three had sunk. In addition to Dominique, a Swiss had abandoned his yacht after it sprang a leak, and Jean Yves Terlain had abandoned the enormous 70-foot catamaran *Kriter III,* which, as *British Oxygen,* had won the Round Britain Race two years before. It too had sprung a leak in the storms. Mike Richey, in *Jester,* was one of those who had retired and, typically, he gave no reasons like "gear failure" for his arrival in Ireland, but merely said that enough was enough and he thought a cruise in the Emerald Isle would be a very much more sensible way to spend his summer holiday.

It was difficult to tell Jack where I was because, after drifting for 15 hours in the storm, I didn't have a very firm idea. I gave my position as the same as the previous day's, which put me 1,000 miles along my track after ten days at sea. Despite everything I was maintaining my 100-miles a day average, but now I was hoarding it with no miles to spare.

Although the boat was still well-heeled over, and work in the galley was difficult, I was determined to finish the day with a hot meal. Onions, tomatoes, herbs, and mushrooms went into a rich sauce for a bowlful of spaghetti. As usual I could manage only half of it, but I had eaten more that day than any other day and I was confident that the Lurgy had finally passed. My body must have adapted to the strange hours I kept and given up expecting sleep, food, or rest at anything but the most unlikely of times. I had always been confident I would start eating again, but I was still very relieved to know it had happened at last. I remained very tired from the previous day's acrobatics over the stern and I needed plenty of good food to recover. I only wished there was an indefatigable cook strapped permanently to the galley. And a washing machine in the cockpit.

At two the next morning I came nearest to sorting out all my problems by slipping in the companionway and falling across the cabin so that my head slammed into the side of the boat. The boat was all right, but it was some time before I knew that I was. Stars and flashing lights spun in front of my eyes and humming filled my ears. For a while I had no idea of where I was, or what had happened. But then I became aware that I was crumpled in a heap in the corner of the chart table. My head was jammed up against the off-course calculator and my nose was being squashed by a rubber flashlight. I tried moving and decided that my skull was probably in one piece, but one wouldn't know it from the amount of pounding and throbbing it was doing. I was all right, but I had been lucky. I should have known better than to go for a look up top wearing only slippery socks on my feet, and I gave my boots a severe ticking off for not having accompanied me.

The next day was cloudy and rainy, which was nothing new, but it was another day when I would have no precise idea of where I was. For the past few days the sun had either been, hidden behind low clouds or it had shone while the wind was throwing up large seas, and it is nothing short of impossible to take a sun sight from a small yacht in those conditions. The horizon may show itself once in a while, but never at the same time as you corner the sun in the sextant's mirror, if you ever find it at all. Working a sextant in bad weather is similar to balancing an egg on a knife while riding a roller coaster.

Not knowing my position was no worry because, even if I were miles out on my dead reckoning, I couldn't be anywhere near land. But I had the nasty feeling I was still miles too far to the north and wanted to find out exactly how much.

As if in answer to my request, a ship happened along. I was down in the cabin when it approached but suddenly and with extraordinary certainty, I knew it was there. I think it must have been the proximity of hot baths, warm food, and human company. I came up quickly and there was the Canadian ship *CP Trader*. Hoping she had seen me I turned on the VHF short-range radio and gave her a call. A British voice replied straightaway and soon gave me my position, which was all I had feared — too far to the north and pushed well back by the storm. The radio operator also gave me a weather forecast and offered to report me to Lloyds. These preliminaries over, we then had a good chat. The ship was bound for Europe out of the Straits of Belle Isle and he told me they had lain hove to for 12 hours in the storm. He was anxious to know how we had got on in the bad weather and how many were we and so on. I told him that "we" were fine and that actually there weren't that many of us, just me, to be precise. This met with a long pause, and finally a hesitant query. I was a girl wasn't I? And I was alone? "Blimey," said the operator, "if you have to go this far to escape the men, you must be ruddy gorgeous."

Just as well he couldn't see me; my spikes had reappeared and my shape was completely obscured by thick clothing, so that I looked about as gorgeous as an angry turnip. But it was a delightful compliment anyway and I glowed and smiled like a starlet at a film premiere.

The weather forecast they gave me also made me happy, for there was not a gale or a depression in sight, which made a nice change, and I felt sure it was safe to look forward to a few days of drier sailing.

Apart from a head that was full of beating hammers and a self-steering gear that had more kinks than straight lines, the *Golly* and I were in one piece and undamaged, and that was a remarkable thing in itself. Now there was only another two thirds of the trip to go, and that was only twice as much again as I'd achieved so far. Only!

7

With the passing of the storm, life became drier and quieter, but it was by no means easier. In the bad weather I had left the *Golly* under bare poles or storm sails, but now that the wind had moderated I was back into the sail-changing routine. Most of the time the wind was from the west or southwest and the boat close-hauled. On this point of sailing it was necessary to have exactly the right amount of sail up to make the *Golly* really fly along; too much and she went sideways on her ear, too little and she became sluggish. There was no problem if the wind strength was constant, but it so rarely was. Nor would it have been so bad if I had always made the right sail changes at the right time, but I was a rotten weather prophet and every time I put up a sail to suit a new wind strength, the wind would change its mind and the *Golly* would be sailing like a slug again.

In a light wind it would only take me a few minutes to take one jib off and haul up another, but in anything more than a breeze I came up against the sheer size and bulk of those sails. When lowering one of the big genoas it was almost impossible not to drop some of it into the water where it would drag along like a lead weight. And once retrieved and on deck, the sail would usually do its best to blow over the side again, so that I had to jump on it to hold it down. Many times I sat firmly on top of the sail until I could gather it in under me and push it toward the forehatch.

After I had forced the sail down into the sailbin, I started setting up the new sail. The quickest way of doing this would have been to hank it on while the old was still set. This was marvelous in theory, but it meant a trip up to the bows while the boat was still thundering along at full speed covered in spray. Sitting on the bow hanking on a madly flapping sail was like being caught in a mad elevator with the shower on. One moment I would be suspended many feet up in the air and then the bows would drop away beneath my feet and keep falling until they sank themselves into a wave, throwing a few gallons of water across the deck.

Somehow I always found reasons for not using this quick sail-changing method. I decided it would take me just as long as the other, drier method, or that it was too dangerous (I might get catapulted off the bow) or, as I would repeat to myself, what did a few more minutes matter anyway? Over 3,000 miles, it might mean an extra half day, but that was a small price to pay for staying dry.

Except that I very rarely seemed to stay dry. I took every precaution against getting drenched, but somehow or another I was always being outwitted. This probably had a lot to do with the way I moved about the foredeck, because unless it looked as steady as a rock, I would either crawl across it on hands and knees or shuffle about on my bottom. Neither were very fast modes of travel but they did have the benefit of feeling twice as safe as standing up and wobbling. But, although the *Golly* moved very much slower once the jib was down, she still managed to pick up some water on her bows and swish it across the deck. It was very difficult to overcome one of the basic instincts of sailing and turn my face into the wind, and yet a faceful of water was almost preferable to what happened when I crawled along on hands and knees with my back to the wind. The water would run across the deck and straight up my trouser leg, then as the boat rolled the other way, it would very neatly fill my boot.

Every time I finished a sail change with a squelching boot I made a mental note to shuffle about on my bottom instead. But on the few occasions when I remembered, I wasn't sure it was much better. Instead of a wet foot I got a wet bottom. This resulted from a slight misunderstanding with Henri-Lloyd, the makers of my oilskins. The oilskins were very waterproof and well designed with trousers that came up to the armpits. But when I had tried them on I realized I must have given my 1955 hip measurements because it took me a full five minutes to wiggle into them. This was no good for rapid and panic-struck leaps into oilskins in dead of night. What I wanted was a front opening from the top of the trousers just far enough down to let me get into them; in other words, what I understood to be a fly. Henri-Lloyd had coyly put "For Miss Francis. Trousers with NO FLY," but I wrote and asked if they could please put in a fly after all. The trousers were returned with a fly all right, but it was not the large opening I had expected; instead there was a small four-inch gap where a gentleman would expect to find one. I never dared return the trousers when I remembered what I had written in my covering letter: "When singlehanded I find a fly most useful, particularly when in a hurry." Which was how Joe, my sailmaker, came to extend the fly into a front opening that stretched from crotch to top and how, whenever I sat down, the water shot straight into the opening and turned my paper underpants into a soggy pulp.

Sail changing was not only wet, but also tiring. Once I had prepared a sail for hoisting I had to winch it up really tight then trot back to the cockpit to sheet it in. The sheet winches had three gears, but I only ever used the third and even then there was no easy way to pull in those large genoas; I just had to keep winching until they were hard in. I viewed my bulging muscles with growing anxiety.

Beating hard to windward not only involved a lot of sail handling, but also that life had to be lived at a permanent angle of 30 degrees. When moving about the cabin I came to rely on my arms and, rather like a monkey, would swoop from handhold to handhold until I could fall into my bunk or wedge myself behind the chart table. For some reason the galley was always on the uphill side and cooking became a demanding exercise in juggling and balancing. I once caught a plate of scrambled eggs making straight for the floor and poured it carefully over my lap instead.

Everything took twice as long and was twice as tiring. A lot of energy was needed to keep upright against a heeling and pitching motion and I had no trouble in justifying my natural inclination to lie in my bunk all day. Unfortunately the chores never got done that way and a fascinating book would often be spoiled by a nagging voice that kept saying "What about the washing up? And those unwhipped rope ends?"

"Yes, yes," I would agree. "Quite right. Must get done, mustn't they? I'll just finish this chapter . . . ."

"Excuse me," said this voice some time later, "but that's two and a half chapters now and . . . ."

"Goodness," I would reply. "How extraordinary! On my way right now. I'll just finish this interesting bit . . . ."

But one chore I didn't put off was the repair of the mast leak for the simple reason that I couldn't ignore it. I would be reading the riveting bit where the antihero doesn't get his girl, when a bolt of water would shoot wetly across the cabin and land on my bunk. The cause of the leak was only too obvious when I looked on deck. The rim that edged the mast hole was fastened down by a number of screws. But now, every single one of these screws lay neatly beside its hole, leaving plenty of channels for water to shoot down into the cabin below. It looked as if someone had come along and carefully unscrewed each one and put it on one side, but I realized it must have been the violent vibration of the mast in the storm that had worked each one loose and pitched it out onto the deck. Fortunately the mast box had prevented the screws from being washed away and I did not have to search for replacements.

Working the radio was never a chore, although it took longer and longer to get through. I never seemed to tune in at a moment when Portishead was listening for calls and often had to sit through several long conversations between oil rigs or Greeks who had apparently not heard news of each other for years. When Portishead finally asked for calls, I would speak eagerly into the handset, only to find that I had been drowned out by a big ship. In this way the large ships always got in ahead of me and it was only after they had finished booking their calls that my signal could be heard. Although Portishead would often try to transfer me to a less busy frequency, I got used to being toward the end of a line and would book my calls correspondingly early.

There was one call that I was very anxious to get through on time, because if I were too late, the pub would be closed. The Travellers Rest, ably run by Stan and Win, was our local and I had promised Stan I would try to call at 9:30 on Wednesday, June 16. Jacques would be there, of course, and my sister, Annie, and her husband, Archie. It would be a tremendous occasion, not only because I would be able to talk to everyone, but also because I could open the little bottle of something that Stan had given me and join in the party. But in my anxiety to get through on time I found myself talking to Stan ten minutes early and no one else had arrived. I was disappointed at missing Jacques and my sister and kicked myself for not having postponed the call. It was great fun talking to Stan, but I had been looking forward to hearing all the family news and after I had rung off I felt letdown and suddenly very tired.

The next day I had another radio schedule: this time with Ron and Joan on the *QE2*. I reckoned that the ship should be within a few hundred miles of me and asked Portishead if they knew her actual position. In their usual helpful way, Portishead did better than that; they established contact with the ship and linked us up. Soon Ron's cheerful voice was saying "Marvelous! You're doing brilliantly! Jet propelled!" and I couldn't help laughing. Ron would have been optimistic and enthusiastic if I were still off the Lizard. I had a few words with Joan, and after ordering an enormous meal for my first evening in Newport, I said good-bye, adding that I was sure they must be having a miserable time on the *QE2*, but they should bear it as best they could.

The thought of the world's most luxurious liner only 60 miles away did turn my imagination toward hot baths and five-course dinners, but comforts apart, I was quite happy in my small world aboard the *Golly* and had no wish to swap boats. And this was just as well because I would look a sorry sight in public. I got out a mirror and, although I was expecting the worst, I was pretty horrified by what I saw. It was time for another wash and shampoo, although I wasn't too enthusiastic about the wash. It meant standing shivering by the sink with a washcloth and a kettle of hot water and not getting very much washed anyway. And after all, who was there to know? In the end I washed my hair, dabbed at my neck, and canceled the rest.

Finding a change of clothes was much more difficult. I had dried out many of the salty ones, but whenever the atmosphere was even slightly damp and that was all the time, the salt reabsorbed the moisture and the clothes became as cold and clammy as before. I had one dry polar suit — a warm woolly sort of fur coat worn inside out — and this I wore down in the cabin when I needed warmth, changing into my next least damp clothes for trips on deck. But the constant changing in and out of damp clothes had me shivering all the time and finally I did what I should have done days before: I used some freshwater to rinse out two sets of clothes and put them out in the cockpit whenever there was a suitable drying day.

Once I had summoned the willpower to do it, I got tremendous satisfaction out of puttering around the boat doing the day's work. But the one job I always found difficult was the filming for the BBC. Out of a sense of discipline that I can only have learned from my training at the Royal Ballet School, I had forced myself to take a film nearly every day, including the times when it had been blowing a gale. Bob Saunders had asked specially for heavy weather sequences because, as he knew from previous sailing films, they were the shots that everyone least wanted to take and every audience most wanted to see.

During the storm there was no way I was going to stroll around fixing cameras on the stern, so I compromised by pointing the camera at a few waves and recording a separate commentary. But as usual, the filming was never as straightforward as it might have been. Something always went wrong. If I didn't forget to plug something in, then the tape recorder started on one of its whining sessions. I would be saying something riveting like "Ahmmm," when the sound of a screeching cat would drown my voice out, and I would have to start looking for the cause of the problem all over again. But the worst of constantly having to replay the tapes was having to listen to my own voice. It was decidedly odd to hear myself talking to no one in particular in the middle of the Atlantic, and in a manner reminiscent of my old history teacher who referred to every event, including the mauling of the early Christians, as "frightfully interesting."

By the twelfth day I was 1,200 miles out from Plymouth and I felt reasonably confident that I would reach the Half-way Stage on the fourteenth day, just on target. Of course this thought was a great mistake; the wind immediately fell light and, after a few last dying breaths, we were becalmed. But it made a nice change from being hard on the wind and I was happy enough to be able to move around without having to swing by my arms. However, I was not so happy to see what the calm had brought. A damp, dripping fog had stolen down and the boat was enclosed in a soundless gray blanket. Fog is eerie at the best of times, but there was something particularly strange about being enveloped in a small, walled world a thousand miles out in the middle of the ocean.

For seven hours the *Golly* rolled gently in the swell, her spars dripping with moisture and her mainsail streaked with rivers of water. The fog was impenetrable and, although I peered into it from time to time, I could see nothing but weird and frail shapes that my eyes conjured up from the shadows. The longer I looked, the more shapes I thought I saw, so I dragged my eyes away and concentrated on using my "little black box," the radar detector. This was a much better indicator of the presence of ships and together with the large radar reflector I had hoisted up the backstay when the fog came down, it should keep me safe from collision.

In 12 days I had seen one ship so I could not believe collision was an enormous risk. On the Azores route I had seen about one ship per day, and sometimes it had resembled Piccadilly Circus with three ships in sight simultaneously, but up here no one seemed to like it very much and with this climate I knew why. The main New York-Europe shipping lane ran to the south, skirting a safe distance around the iceberg limits, and the only ships that ventured farther north were those bound for nothern ports who were prepared to navigate the fog and ice.

Not to say I did not keep a reasonable lookout, but as time went on and the ocean seemed emptier and emptier, I peered out only once an hour and sometimes even less. But I did carry a white masthead light at night, which was more than many others did. This was no good in fog, of course, but in good visibility there was some hope of it being seen.

These precautions were all I could reasonably take, but I knew that I could still be run down. It would take no more that 20 minutes for a fast ship to appear over the horizon and hit me, so I might easily never see it on one of my routine lookouts. The odds of being hit were thousands, or even millions to one, I was not sure which, but then I was never impressed by these figures anyway. Either there was a ship with my number on it or there wasn't. I had a nice feeling there wasn't, which was just as well, because otherwise I would be having a miserable time.

More worrying was the possibility of an iceberg with my number on it.

Icebergs did not carry radar and were often shrouded in fog. But the icebergs, if there were any, would be a long way ahead, near the Grand Banks of Newfoundland, so it was a bit early to worry about them. Yet that fog had a dank coldness that made me think of ice and great arctic wastes.

I had a good shiver and reminded myself that this could not possibly be the beginning of the Newfoundland fog, which was still days away. And as if to confirm it, a breeze came up from the south and blew it away. Confident that I wouldn't see any more fog for a while, I took down the radar reflector and put my little black box away. It was a classic situation for "Sod's Law" and no sooner had I written "Fog's blown away" in my logbook than I looked up to see that it was back again. I wrote, "A slight mist has appeared," put up the radar reflector, and turned on the little black box as if I'd never put them away.

Coming so soon after the bad weather this fog was not giving me much of a chance to fix my position. The *Golly* was fitted with a battery of Brookes and Gatehouse instruments that were worthy of a Concorde's flight deck. There was a log or distance meter, an electronically read compass and, using the data from these two, a distance-off-course computer. This computer told me how many miles to port or starboard I had strayed from my desired course, which I had preset on the compass. There was also a wind speed and direction indicator with numerous repeaters in the cockpit, a small radio receiver on which I listened for weather forecasts and ships talking on the marine band. It also served as a radio direction finder in coastal waters. Finally there was a depth sounder, not very useful here where it was several miles deep, but very nice to have all other times.

But these instrumennts, though magnificent, were only as good as "the idiot who used them," as the saying went. Without a sun sight it was impossible to put an X on the chart and say with any certainty that one was definitely there, for there was nothing definite about it at all. Errors crept in everywhere: from not using the instruments properly, from not allowing enough for current or leeway, and from not knowing where you were in the first place. This was my main problem. I had got a position from the Canadian ship two days before, but that was the only fix I had received in five days, and my area of possible position had spread to an area of about 50 square miles, quite large by any standards.

When the fog lifted the next day and revealed a watery sun, I could hardly believe it and picking up my sextant and chronometer, I leaped into the cockpit at a speed that was unusual for me. Now, at last, I would find out where I was for sure! I took several sights, carefully noted the exact time, and hurried below to work them out. Then I double-checked them for elementary mathematical errors, which often seemed to turn up in my calculations, and plotted the results on the chart.

To this day I can't work out what had happened. But there was no doubt about it. Either the log distance was underreading by a large margin, or else I had misheard the position from the Canadian ship, but I was much farther west than I had thought. This was pleasant news, but still disconcerting. How could I be so far out? Working forward from my last known position before the storm, it was possible I was where the sun sight now put me. But working forward from the ship's position, it was impossible. Despite the many tales expert navigators tell of knowing their positions better than the ships they meet, I could not believe that a ship with all the modern navigational aids could be mistaken. And yet something very strange had occurred. I took many more sights that day and checked the sextant and chronometer for error, but there was no doubt of my position.

Nor was there any doubt I was still too far north. Although I had taken every opportunity to claw south, I had not achieved as much as I had hoped for. I wanted to pass over the south of the Grand Banks and then south of Sable Island to avoid fishing boats and the worst of the ice and fog, and generally to keep clear of land. But it was proving to be a battle and I was beginning to wish I had taken the Rhumb Line course, a slightly longer route but ideal for the south-westerlies that were blowing. According to the wind chart, I could have expected westerly winds to blow just as often as these sou'westers, but they never did. Instead the wind would come up from the south, as it had the day before, and then settle slightly south of southwest so that I could almost lay my course — but not quite. And the not quite was always pushing me north.

I had a long talk with my parents that evening. Father was able to tell me all about the bad weather we'd been having, and from the way he talked, he was becoming quite an expert. Later I heard that Father's office in London frequently came to a standstill while he peered out of the window and looked at the sky above New Broad Street, muttering beneath his breath. And it was said he'd walked past several acquaintances in the street, his attention captured by some fascinating altocumulus blowing in from the west.

My parents also gave me news of other competitors. It seemed I was doing quite well in relation to the other Jester Class boats and even to the large boats. I didn't find out until later, but I was at that stage only 180 miles behind the eventual winner, Eric Tabarly in *Pen Duick VI*. There had been nearly 30 retirements, including several of the Azores Race competitors. Chris Smith in the tiny 22 ½-foot *Tumult* had returned to England and who could blame him. Angus Primrose had been completely rolled over and his boat dismasted, so that he was limping back to England under jury rig. Other boats had capsized, rolling over 90 degrees or more, several had sprung leaks, and a total of five had sunk, fortunately with no loss of life. I was beginning to realize how lucky I had been to escape the gales with only a damaged self-steering gear, and one that had been repairable at that. There was news of Aline Marchand, who was doing well, but nothing had yet been heard from the splendid Ida, who was doubtless too busy speaking torrential Italian to her instruments to talk with ships.

There were many boats that were unsighted, but this was no cause for concern. Without a radio transmitter it was almost impossible to communicate with ships, even if they came close enough to see you. If you started signaling by semaphore they would think you were probably mad, and you would feel it too, standing there waving your arms like a demented scarecrow. And if you started signaling the Morse code with a torch you might just have time to send your boat's name before the ship was over the horizon. If it was a fine day you could always shout, but if the ship was that close, it was usually to say something unfriendly.

After the calm, the wind had been light for a good 12 hours, which allowed me a rare chance to cook a large meal, read a good book, and have a relaxed sleep. But the forecast gave southwest Force 6 - 8 and I was soon sweating away at the sail changes again as the wind freshened. I couldn't believe there was another gale on its way. I made the necessary preparations anyway, and reduced sail in plenty of time, which usually is a wise thing to do. This time the wind never increased beyond Force 6, instead it blew for half an hour, moderated and then blew again. I was up and down like a yo-yo — fighting sails on the foredeck, resting in a heap in the cockpit, and then back into the fray again, still panting from the last effort. Whenever I had got the right amount of sail up, it would be wrong. The wind thoroughly outsmarted me on every occasion. Even when I tried a double-bluff and left too little sail up hoping that the wind would increase again, it didn't. Not until I had waited two hours and put up a larger sail, that is. My biceps ached with the effort and I could see them growing in front of my very eyes.

There was still fog about and I made yet another entry in my log concerning "thick mist," adding, "I hope this doesn't last all the way to Newport." I had the uncomfortable memory of saying something ashore about "I'm expecting gales for the first half and fog for the second, then I won't be disappointed." Trouble was, the second half of the trip was going to start the very next day, and I had the feeling I was going to be very disappointed indeed.

The next day I wrote in my log, "Well, I *think* I'm halfway!" The wind had come around to the west, then continued to veer to the northwest so that I could sail free at last. But that northwesterly wind also brought a cold, thick fog that sent shivers down my spine, for the harder the wind blew, the thicker the fog became. Fog with wind rarely occurs around the British coast and I found it difficult to adjust to the *Golly* roaring along at seven knots or more, straight into a wall of white. Sometimes I could not see the bow, at other times the fog would swirl far enough away to reveal large waves looming out of nowhere, ghostly shapes that would suddenly appear like lumps of gray rock. After a while I couldn't look anymore — the appearance of each lump made me jump and, rather than give myself a nervous day, I went below and read the information on fog to see if it offered any encouragements.

I found that the *Pilot* was quite lengthy on the subject of fog. The fog over the Grand Banks of Newfoundland was well known for both its density and its frequency. It was caused by the tremendous difference in temperature between the cold water of the Labrador Current and the warm winds that blow off the American Continent. The Labrador Current flows down from the Arctic, along the Labrador Coast and south to Newfoundland, where it turns along the coast of Nova Scotia to New England and is eventually absorbed by the warm Gulf Stream.

From its origins in the Arctic the current brings freezing water that meets the warm continental air, condenses it, and forms fog. But that is not all it brings. When the ice at the fringe of the Arctic starts to break up in spring, icebergs and growlers are also carried south on the current until, by midsummer, there may be hundreds floating around the Grand Banks, slowly melting as they meet the warmer water of the Gulf Stream.

I had known that fog was to be expected on the Grand Banks themselves, but I was a bit surprised to find it so dense here, 300 miles to the east. But the wind was blowing straight off the ice so I guessed that the air was too cold for the water. It was certainly too cold for me, and I started my Halfway Day celebrating by putting on two pairs of long johns, two sweaters, and a thick woolly hat. I then lit the heater, which promptly exploded back into the cabin. It probably didn't like the cold wind either.

Once I was warm, I felt much more cheerful and was determined to enjoy my Halfway Day. I would get all the chores finished by midmorning, I would have a light lunch, I would read a good book, and I would then eat myself into the ground over a three-course feast, falling onto my bunk in a stupor at dusk. It would be a perfect day.

But there were two things that were worrying me. One was the icebergs, which might have drifted much farther east than anyone thought. And the second was my hairbrush, which I couldn't find anywhere. Spikes were bad enough, but the thought of having unbrushed ones made my hair stand on end.

8

If I were to get the chores finished by midmorning I would have to get started straightaway. I lay in my bunk a while and planned my strategy. I would get the unpleasant jobs over with first and work toward the enjoyable ones. That meant starting with the washing up, the filming, the cleaning, and going on to the cooking, the eating, the navigation, and the radio.

I read a chapter of Chichester's *Along the Clipper Way* to give my mind a rest, then rolled out of my bunk to have a look on deck. There was nothing but a white blanket as usual, although it looked a bit thinner than before. I switched on the black box, turned it through 360 degrees so that its sensor arm had a complete sweep of the horizon, and when it reported no ships, I turned it off. I then checked our course, the wind speed, and the trim of the sails. A quick look at the self-steering gear, always half frightened of what I might see, and I had finished my routine checks. Now for the washing up, which sat in a small canvas bucket in the cockpit. It would take only a minute to do it with some fresh seawater and then it would be over for another two days, or even three if I reused the same knives and forks and ate off paper plates.

But it was so cold! I really had to get warm and hit on the idea of returning to my bunk until I had stopped shivering. Another few pages of *Along the Clipper Way* and I began thawing out. A quick half-hour snooze, and I began getting warm. Then it was time for another look on deck, and I had to get warm all over again.

At ten o'clock I firmly and finally decided to start on the chores and leaped up, full of enthusiasm. But I wasn't too happy about the order I was going to do them in. I really should *start* with the radio and work back to the washing up. The dirty dishes could wait forever, but there might be a ship passing within radio range at that very moment. I wanted to call a passing ship to ask for iceberg information and assuming the news would be favorable, I could then have an enjoyable Halfway Day with only my lost hairbrush to worry about.

I turned on the main engine to produce plenty of power for the transmitter, warmed up the set, and started calling on the international calling frequency. When I got an immediate response I was surprised; I had imagined that it would take some time to contact a ship, there being so few about. But my pleasure at finding a ship so quickly was shortlived; his signal was weak and his voice covered in crackle and interference. And, what was worse, he had a thick foreign accent, which meant we were going to have a long and difficult conversation.

We exchanged boat's names, although I didn't quite catch his, and then I explained that I needed ice information. Did he have any? Please, came the reply, what information did I want? Ice, I said. I - C - E. Ah, he said, no, he only wished he had it would be useful, wouldn't it? Must be hearing things, I thought . . . a strange ship that didn't have any ice information around these frozen wastes. Did he have no idea at all? I pressed. Sorry, no understand, came the reply. At which I gave up and asked for weather information; did he have any?

please repeat, came the reply. Wea - th - er, I said slowly. Ah, weather! Oh no, he said, only what one heard on the BBC. I was just thinking how very remarkable this ship was, when the voice went on to ask me if I knew where I was, because if I did I was very lucky. He himself had not the faintest idea, having not seen the sun for days.

At this point a vague suspicion began to enter my mind. Just a small notion that this might not actually be a ship at all. I asked if he would kindly repeat his ship's name. Back it came: "Spaniel." A hasty look down the list of competitors and I had got it. Entry number 110, *Spaniel,* sailed by Kazimierz Jaworski for Poland.

I suppose it was possible for me to have been denser, but it would have been difficult. I apologized for asking all the stupid questions, gave my position, and told the Pole all the news I had heard from England. He told me where he thought he was, which was to the south and just ahead of me, and said, yes he would very much like to have his position reported to London. With a "Good luck" and "See you in Newport" we then said good-bye. The poor fellow must have thought I was mad.

I looked at his position on the chart. It was just where I wanted to be, farther south. and of course he was a few miles ahead of me. But I took this to be a great encouragement. *Spaniel* was the same size as the *Golly,* so I must be keeping reasonably well up with some of the Jester Class boats at least. Doubtless the large boats were a long way ahead, but I hardly felt we were in the same race with them, so it didn't bother me.

If I had known that I was lying fourth overall, that apart from *Spaniel,* there were only *Pen Duick VI* and *Club Méditerranée* ahead of me, I might have felt differently. Certainly I would have been surprised. Of course Jack Hill and my family were constantly telling me how brilliantly I was doing, but I couldn't help thinking they were a little bit prejudiced and took their wildly enthusiastic comments with a large pinch of salt. I was quite happy to think I was somewhere in the middle of the fleet and wasn't going to disgrace the ladies of Britain.

Half an hour after my interesting talk with *Spaniel,* I tried calling "All ships" again. This time I got a call from a vessel called the *Ardestove,* or that's what it sounded like. After a quick look down the competitors list, I was fairly confident I was talking to a ship at last, but just to be sure I asked him for his position and when he answered with certainty I knew he couldn't be one of us. The ship was Norwegian and we had some language difficulties, but eventually he was able to tell me that, although there were icebergs ahead, they were to the north and south and not directly in my path.

This was good news and I settled down to enjoy my day with more confidence. And to cheer me up completely, the fog drifted away until I could see the horizon and overhead, low gray clouds, a welcome sight for once.

Meals were infinitely flexible on board the *Golly* and their timing depended on when I, the cook, felt like making the effort to wedge myself beside the cooker and grapple with some ingredients. Or when that was too much, to grasp a tin opener and eat straight from the tin. Breakfast happened any time between 7 A.M. and midday, depending on whether I was keeping local Atlantic time or British time and I was never sure which I preferred. By way of celebration I decided to have a three-course English breakfast. My stomach not being used to large quantities of food, this would take me at least three hours to eat and would therefore merge very nicely with lunch and save me cooking another meal. I ate a small bowl of *muesli* and long-life milk for my first course, and after half an hour's thought, decided on scrambled eggs and tomatoes on toast for the next. I had plenty of eggs to eat up. I had asked Mother if she could buy me six dozen but she had said something about being on the safe side and, in addition to the six stowed with the fresh provisions, I kept coming across odd boxes of eggs in a number of surprising places — next to the engine, under the sink, and hidden behind the batteries. There was no worry about running out

114

nor was there any danger of the eggs going bad. Knowing that supermarket eggs were two weeks old or more and would not last the race, Mother had hurried off to the local farm and ensured there the eggs' freshness by, as she put it, personally standing under every hen.

Mother had done an excellent job with the fruit and vegetables too. She had bought various batches in different stages of ripeness (I was eating apples, bananas, grapefruit, and even tomatoes until my arrival in Newport). This excellent system of ripening by stages sometimes went wrong. Once I left a whole bunch of bananas too long and had to eat them all at one sitting, like a rapacious baboon. Another time I put my hand into the darker regions of the fresh-food locker and grasped something very unpleasant and very squelchy. Suppressing a scream, I forced myself to pull out the soggy mess and found it to be an unannounced tray of tomatoes.

I was not short of bread either. There were several loaves lining the pilot berth and I knew that somewhere down the quarter berth were another few dozen. The conditions aboard were perfect for the growth of mold (close and damp) and the loaves were invisible in their coats of gray-green. But once this covering was cut away the bread was fresh and soft inside. Delicious with cheese or marmalade or stuffed straight into the mouth.

I sat down to my scrambled egg and tomatoes at lunchtime, having negotiated the various stages of preparation and cookery without losing a single tomato or piece of toast to the cabin floor. My final course, which was marmalade on bread and butter, was eaten at teatime. Marmalade was one thing I had plenty of. Before the race Robertson's had sent a truck loaded with cases of their products to the marina. I had jars of jam, marmalade, and mincemeat, as well as tins of their vegetables and fruit — probably enough to last me a year.

Although I ate a lot of fresh food, I still relied on tins for the fruit juice, which I drank throughout the day, and of course for the plums, which I ate most evenings. But with some concern I noticed that, with the continuous sluicing of the bilge water, all the tins were getting very rusty and my careful ink markings were beginning to disappear. I was not too concerned until I opened a tin of what I thought were "Blk Bris" to find I was pouring custard onto broad beans ("Brd Bns"). I tried remarking some of the tins but never got around to doing the full 150-odd, and was sometimes forced to rely on X-ray eyes and intuition.

When I was halfway through my long breakfast I suddenly decided to brave the cold and have a wash because I knew I wouldn't have the courage to face another for a long time. I had been inspired by one of the contents of the parcel my godmother had given me. It was some Yves St. Laurent talcum powder and, when I sniffed it, it smelled so good that I longed to smell like that too. It was not that I smelled badly — it was just that I could not be put to the acid test of having people sit beside me. I was musty and salty, rather like an ancient sea relic. I longed to feel fresh and vaguely feminine again, although I wondered if I'd still recognize the feeling.

As I washed and powdered myself I was amazed to discover that I had a new body. There were bones and hollows where none had been before. I had always thought my hips were naturally wide, but they were really quite narrow. If I could manage to stay that way my clothes would look marvelous on me. But, with a sigh, I had to admit that a bikini would not look as good because, along with my hips, my bosom had almost entirely disappeared. I hadn't been much of a Jayne Mansfield to start with but I was still a bit put out. It was the principle of the thing.

With so many sharp bones protruding, I was covered in a multitude of bruises that ranged through every color from dirty orange to bright purple. On favorite spots like my knees and thighs they were arranged in clusters like exhibits at a flower show. I was well practiced in moving around the boat carefully, but when every single object was sharp, jutting, or just plain hard, it was impossible to escape them all the time. The worst were the cleats. If they didn't get me on the ankle when I walked by, then they'd bang me on the knee as I crawled past. But it was my shins that had the most painful encounters and always with the sill of the main hatchway, which was both hard and sharp. In bad weather it was impossible not to receive bruises everywhere, for the motion of the boat was too wild to anticipate with any accuracy. It was a matter of clinging on and dodging the bits of boat as they came at you.

After my wash I felt better and even tackled the washing up, an achievement that gave me great satisfaction. Then, to my delight, I saw a watery sun behind the clouds and within two minutes I had taken a sun sight. It was a good feeling to know where I was, particularly when it put me right where I had estimated my position to be. I would have liked to have taken another sight to verify the first, but the cloud thickened again and I saw no more of the sun that day. Navigation was a thing I enjoyed doing so long as the weather was reasonable. If it was rough it took hours of balancing and terrible concentration to get the horizon, the sun, and the sextant to come together. Then I would find that peering through the eyepiece had made me cross-eyed and I was unable to focus on the chronometer. Having missed the precise time I would then have to start all over again. To make matters more difficult my hands had become stiff and swollen with a number of unhealed cuts in the creases of the fingers, so that I was unable to handle the sextant as well as I might.

The working out of the sight was quite simple, although not nearly as simple as people like to make out. It had taken me three years to become really fast at it, but then I had the handicap of being self-taught. I used the "yachtsman's method," which is as short and simple as you can make it, most of the work having been done for you by the Admiralty in the form of precalculated tables. But the thinking behind this method took a bit of getting used to. You had to estimate where you were, then ignore that and imagine you were somewhere nearby, and then find out how far you were from the place you imagined yourself to be but weren't. To ensure that I didn't lose the thread of these calculations I had designed an "idiot-proof" working sheet. This was a standard form with such reminders as "Enter sextant reading here," "ADD here," "Take from 2nd column." At a point where I often made a mistake, I had put "DON'T DO IT."

In the afternoon I had a nap, interspersed by quick looks on deck. If I was very tired I would sleep most of the afternoon, but on a good day I would just rest an hour or two and then do more work around the boat or better still, read. I had a wide variety of books on board, ranging from *War and Peace* to the latest of James Herriot. I had been trying to read *War and Peace* for three years and I was still convinced that a lone voyage must be the ideal place to read it. But, although there was nobody to interrupt me, there was still too much happening to let me concentrate sufficiently. My mind was always half on the boat and what the wind was up to, so I had to have a good simple story that I could leave and return to without losing the gist. The most unsatisfactory book I read was Lawrence's *Women in Love*. I found it so depressing that I had to banish it to the other end of the boat.

I had to take care not to get too excited over a good story. If I became too enthusiastic at turning the pages, the book fell apart in my hands. Some books were wetter than others, but nearly all had transparent print, soggy bindings and, after a time, the musty smell of mildew.

Late on Halfway Day I was still determined to get the unpleasant jobs over with and only three hours behind schedule, I steeled myself to do some filming. The sea was not rough that day so setting up the camera should not require too many acrobatics and cliff-hangings in the area of the stern. Trailing wires, cameras, and plugs I set off in the direction of the camera mount and had soon fixed everything on. I thought how easy it had been for a change and that if I could only get used to the sheer nuisance, time, and effort involved, I might enjoy doing it. Turning away from the stern I then received a wave straight in the chest. Small things get to mean a lot in the confines of a boat, taking on a significance quite out of proportion to their true importance. Although I wasn't sure I considered a wave in the chest to be a small thing at all — in fact it was quite monstrous. And the more I thought about it, the more monstrous it became. The boat had been behaving perfectly well all day, riding the waves like a cork and then, just at the moment that I was exposed on the side deck without oilskins and, I could hardly bear to think of it, wearing my one dry polar suit, up popped this wave and fell on me. It was almost certainly a plot to spoil my day, and I was hot with indignation, stomping and muttering around the boat for a good ten minutes until I had changed into another, almost-dry set of clothes.

Most of the clothes I had rinsed in fresh water were drying well, but just to finish them off, I lit the heater and draped them around the cabin. The newly wet polar suit went through the same process and hung there, dripping like a bear that had just been for a swim. But I hardly needed an excuse to put on the heater anyway — my hands and feet were like ice and I could only get them to thaw out by huddling close to the warmth and steaming gently like a Christmas pudding.

Every few days I would check the fuel and water levels. The heater used kerosene, of which I had more than enough, and the main engine ran on diesel fuel, the supply of which was going to be a tight thing. I ran the engine for one to two hours a day to charge the large bank of batteries necessary to power the transmitter, the masthead light, and the electronic instruments. I had calculated that I should have just enough diesel fuel to last for four weeks using the transmitter for an hour a day. But it had been difficult to estimate the fuel consumption with accuracy, so I checked the contents of the large 12-gallon tank sunk into the keel every three days or so. This involved dipping a cane through a hole on top of the tank, but I was never quite certain of exactly how much fuel I had left. Somehow we had never managed to get the cane marked with the exact quantities, because it would have involved emptying the tank and finding a patient pump operator to fill it gallon by gallon and ignore the hootings of the inevitable line of boats behind.

But if the fuel level was guesswork, the water level was pure intuition. Apart from putting my eye to the hole in the top of the tank, which told me very little, I relied on my own estimate of what I had used. Surprisingly it was never far out and, much later, I ran out on the very day that I thought I might be getting a bit low. I had a six-gallon Jerry can of water for such an emergency, which was sufficient for two weeks' hair washing and face desalting. I never worried about drinking water. I could always catch enough rain or dripping fog for that.

That afternoon as I put the dip into the fuel tank and wondered if the 8 I had marked on it meant eight used or eight to go, I heard a high-pitched squeaking through the hull.

Dolphins are the most talkative of creatures and cannot come and play by a boat without telling their friends what fun it is. Their high-pitched squeaks are quite unmistakable and, whenever I heard them, I would hurry on deck to watch them swooping and diving around the bows. Their favorite game was "chicken." Two dolphins would rush at the *Golly* from the opposite sides, dive under the keel, and see who gave way first. At least that's what I imagined they did, for they would come up to the surface, chatter for a moment, and then shoot off to play the game again.

But when the dolphins came I hardly dared look astern for, following on behind, there would often be those ponderous and slavish creatures, the pilot whales. The textbook I had brought said nothing about whales and dolphins keeping company with each other, yet it seemed too much of a coincidence that they should appear together so often. That day was no exception and I saw the dark, blunt shapes of the whales diving and surfacing slowly in the wake. This time they seemed to be closer than ever and I couldn't help feeling a little nervous. They were quite different from the dolphins. They were larger and jet black all over, with square, almost humped noses. They moved slowly but purposefully and I had the impression, once again, that they thought the *Golly* might be their leader. I just hoped they would not come any closer to find out, or worse, that one of them decided the *Golly* was the only girl he'd ever loved.

Despite my enormous breakfast I had my heart set on a large and disgusting feast by way of a celebration dinner. Traditionally this feast was to consist of the most fattening and unhealthy dishes I could think of because on land such food makes me sick and fat and gives me indigestion — to name a few — while at sea I could get away with this piggish behavior without any side effects at all.

Since teatime somehow had merged into supper, I found that, unintentionally, my first course was a slice of rich fruit cake. But soon I got into my dinner proper with a large bowl of spaghetti and rich tomato sauce with plenty of garlic. My stomach stuck out like a football and I had to stagger to my bunk to recover. But after a while visions of pudding started to enter my mind. It was a tradition that I finished celebration feasts with candied chestnuts and cream, and Mother and I had laid in a good store of both in the Treats Locker. After scraping away some rust to read the markings, I soon found the appropriate tins and started to open them, my mouth watering with greed. The next moment I stared, then tasted, then stared again. The chestnuts were unsweetened and, even worse, mashed up into a puree — ideal for savory stuffings, but not for pudding. I was very disappointed and searched through the Treats Locker, but all the tins marked "Chstnts" looked identical in size and shape, so I didn't bother to open them. This was a real blow and I had to console myself with a large tin of plums and custard.

This finished me off very nicely and I lay in my bunk glowing with contentment, happily listening to music from a tape recorder. I had a collection of about 40 tapes, along with a small cassette player that plugged into the radio's loudspeaker. But I was now using the BBC's tape recorder to play my music. I had requisitioned it after my own stopped working. At first I couldn't think what the problem could be, but after opening the case and finding every moving part firmly immobilized by rust, I realized that three ocean crossings had been more that enough for it.

By the time I had listened to Handel's *Water Music* (a present from my godmother) and Debussy's *La Mer* (a present from Mother), I was ready to sleep. Generally I went to sleep when it got dark, at about ten o'clock Atlantic time. Just before I turned in I would switch on the masthead light, have a quick look on deck and around the horizon, and set up the spare compass beside my bunk. I always slept on the leeward, or lower bunk of the two settee berths in the main cabin, so that I couldn't fall out. Although the quarter berth was nearer the companionway and the instruments, it was difficult to get in and out of it quickly, and I preferred the settee berths where I could roll out and be on my feet within moments. By leaning my head over the edge of the berth I could also see the spare compass and check that we were still on course without having to go on deck every time. In fog I worked the little black box from the bunk too so that, unless there was some sail changing or trimming to be done, I need not go on deck at all.

Most nights I would wake every hour or so, roll out, stumble up on deck, and look around. There were never any ships, but there was often sail trimming, or worse, sail changing to be done. But once back in my sleeping bag I would drop straight off to sleep again as if I'd never been up. I could never do it on land, but it was easy at sea. The physical tiredness blotted out any thoughts that might keep me awake and, after the initial complaints, my body got used to my strange nocturnal habits.

Not surprisingly, waking up and going on deck were never so easy as falling asleep again. Worry about ships was the greatest inducement to look around, followed shortly by anxiety about an indefinable something. I was never sure what this something might be, possibly a piece of jetsam or a whale or a giant squid with arms 50 feet long that was about to pull the boat down. But something always made me roll out, get up, and take a look until doing so became an automatic reflex. But I needed no help to wake myself up when the wind changed strength. With a sense that always stayed awake I could feel changes in the boat's motion and speed, and would slowly become aware that I needed to put up more or less sail. If the wind increased I would reduce sail in no time, but if it decreased I would have great debates as to whether I was going to ignore the fact or not. Sloth usually won the argument and I would make up the most elaborate excuses for putting it off — like "wind's bound to get up again," "won't make any difference over 3,000 miles," and "I don't care anyway!"

One of Ron's presents to the boat had been a kitchen timer, and it was this I used to wake me every hour, although I had a talent for sleeping through it when I really put my mind to it. There was also an off-course alarm attached to the off-course computer. This device was most ingenious. It could be set to ring at various degrees off course and with varying sensitivity and it was the only sure way of knowing that, led by the self-steering, the boat had followed a change in the wind direction. But there was one problem. My nerves couldn't stand all the ringing and pinging. There I'd be, just settling into my sleeping bag with the prospect of an hour's uninterrupted sleep when I'd find that my eyes were staring at the woodwork. Jamming them shut, I'd then listen to my nerves jarring like chalk on a blackboard. "Now stop this," I'd say to myself, "of course that alarm isn't about to go off; just forget about it." Eventually I'd doze off into an uneasy sleep, whereupon a halyard would slap against the mast. Suddenly I'd be wide awake and bolt upright listening for some dreaded sound above the racket of my heartbeat. Then I'd remember that the sound I was dreading was only the alarm and, groaning, would lie back and try to sleep again. Five minutes later the alarm would sound. Bolt upright, heart pounding nerves jangling like piano strings, I would stand up to find I had no knees, only jelly. Staggering to the alarm I would switch it off, put the boat back on course, and ooze back into my bunk like a runny cheese. "Haven't you forgotten something?" some voice would say. "Absolutely not," I would reply. "But the alarm . . . shouldn't you put it back on?" By that time I didn't need to reply, because, with nerves relaxed and eyes like weights, I had fallen into a deep sleep.

Although I became used to getting up every hour there was one aspect of interrupted sleep that I never became accustomed to and that was the vividness of my interrupted dreams. As my sleep became deeper through the night, so my dreams became even more graphic and technicolored — epic dramas that had me on the edge of my seat. Between the instant of hearing the timer go off and waking, I would find myself hanging off cliffs, being chased by monsters or, worst of all, reliving my most embarrassing moment. So real were some of these dreams that they would reverberate around my brain for hours, even days afterwards and I would have the unpleasant feeling I was living several lives at once.

But the night of my Halfway Day provided a relatively pleasant dream to remember and relive the next day. I was lying on a comfortable bed of cushions on a sunny terrace, warm and content, and absolutely full after the most gargantuan feast of all the dishes I most love in the world. I was thinking how perfect life was when a waiter entered bearing an enormous tin of sweet chestnuts that he poured into a bowl at my feet and covered with cream. Despite my full stomach I conveniently discovered I had plenty of room for the contents of this bowl and probably another two as well. As I shoveled spoon after spoon into my mouth, the waiter held up a giant hairbrush, as tall as he was. "It was in your handbag all the time," he said.

But when I looked the next morning I was most disappointed to find it wasn't there at all.

9

As I approached the Grand Banks it became bitterly cold. It was as if the wind had blown out of an enormous refrigerator. I could almost feel the arctic ice in its breath. There was a different smell in the air too, a strong scent of fish and decaying sea life, carried down with the melting ice.

As always there was fog. Sometimes it would fade a little, but then it would swoop down as thick as ever, and we would be sailing into a white curtain again. I tried not to peer ahead too often because all I could see were the hundreds of icebergs my eyes conjured up and my nerves couldn't stand the strain.

The place had a terrible emptiness to it, a desolation that entered one's bones with every blast of icy wind. I had a strong impression of space and distance and for once I was aware of how very far from land we were. Normally I never thought beyond the three miles of water I could see around me, a miniature world across which the *Golly* seemed to be sailing forever. But here, I was aware of what I was, a small person in the middle of a large ocean. And it was a cold and lonely feeling.

Loneliness was not something I often experienced at sea. I missed people, which is an entirely different thing, for it has the promise of reunion and plenty of human company in the future. Also, the boat and the sea were familiar old friends and, until either gave me cause to believe otherwise, I felt safe in their company. I have only felt real loneliness in big cities or other places where there are plenty of people about but no one to talk to. Normally I dislike being alone and if there are people around I will always seek them out. But here there was not much chance of finding someone to talk to, so I didn't feel I was missing anything. It was the difference between going for a walk on your own with the prospect of seeing the family for tea and coming home to a silent and empty house to find a note stuck on the door: "Gone to a party — you're invited too!" but no indication as to where the party might be.

Out here in the deathly quiet and dank fog, I suddenly wanted to be where I was sure everyone else must be — in the warm and sunny ocean to the south. For a moment I even imagined I had been sucked hundreds of miles to the north and it was only by frequent looks at the compass and chart that I convinced myself I was heading south of Newfoundland.

The best remedy for loneliness and thoughts of the Arctic was to keep myself occupied, but even when busy down in the cabin, I felt an eerie atmosphere that made me shiver. Not that I wasn't shivering anyway. However many clothes I put on, I was still cold. I must have looked like an overweight teddy bear, and I certainly felt it as I rolled around the boat, bouncing off the bulkheads. I wore so many layers that my arms stuck out from my sides as if my deodorant had turned to concrete. On top of a vest and paper panties I wore Mother's thermonuclear underwear consisting of silky long johns and top, then a polar suit made of thick tufted wool like a fur coat turned inside out, and finally a pair of old jeans and two very baggy sweaters. On my head I wore a wool balaclava and around my neck a towel. When going on deck I would put oilskins on top of all this, although it was a tremendous effort to haul them on and resulted in much puffing and panting. But after I had been sail changing or winching for a while I would regret nearly every layer of clothing. Within minutes I would be dying of heat, and inside my super-efficient oilskins it felt like a hothouse —very warm, very humid, and very uncomfortable.

But while my body was burning hot, my hands were freezing. The one thing I had forgotten was gloves. Not that I could wear them to handle the ropes, but it would have been nice to keep my hands warm between sail changes so that they wouldn't freeze so quickly on deck. My fingers were already cracked and swollen from heaving on sails and lines and now they were cold as well; it was all I could do to grasp a halyard.

Once, as I was sitting on deck sucking and blowing on my fingers, waiting for them to thaw out and allow me to finish a sail change, it occurred to me that I was either on the wrong route or mad. It was midsummer and if I were only a few miles to the south I could be lying under a burning hot sun, frying my skin to a turn, and sipping a gin on the afterdeck. Instead, here I was, doing my best to impersonate a polar bear, not only in appearance, but also in habitat.

And what was more, I was tired and fed up. After 17 days of sail grappling, being thrown around, and not getting any sleep, I suddenly decided that I was very tired indeed and didn't feel prepared to face another of those killing sail changes. Far from getting more practiced at dropping the genoas neatly, I seemed to throw them over the side all the time. And sitting on the lowered sail didn't appear to impress the wind — it would blow into a fold of the canvas and form a balloon that grew and grew until the sail billowed up into a small spinnaker. When I jumped on it or grabbed at it or lay on it, the balloon would only reappear elsewhere. After much grappling I would eventually persuade the sail to bunch itself up and disappear down the forehatch, only to face the same kind of undisciplined behavior from the next sail when I pulled that up on deck. There was one sail, the Number One genoa, that was particularly heavy and unbending and it took all my strength to move it about. I didn't bother to bag that sail because I could never have lifted it up in one piece. Instead I left it loose in the sailbin so that I could pull it up section by section. With hands that would hardly grip, this was a real struggle.

Neither was sail hoisting and winching any easier than it had been when I was afflicted by the Lurgy. My hands complained bitterly at contact with the ropes and I didn't seem to have the energy to wind on the winches. I had always winched in the large genoas in easy stages — getting some sail in, then resting, pulling a little more and another pause, and then, if the last few inches were impossible, I would head the *Golly* into the wind to take the pressure off the sail and quickly winch in the rest. But now it wasn't weakness that made it difficult, it was a deep tiredness and, I had to admit, a general lack of enthusiasm.

When the wind dropped to a light breeze, it was necessary to replace the wind vane on the self-steering with a larger, lighter one to prevent the gear from becoming sluggish. Changing vanes normally took me a moment, but now my cold hands fumbled and failed to grip and suddenly the light vane was over the side and floating in the wake. I knew I could go back for it and, as I kept telling myself, I really *should*. And yet, as I watched it disappearing fast behind, I knew I wouldn't be turning the boat around. There was something repugnant about turning back the way I had come, even for a few minutes, and as the vane disappeared into the fog I was rather relieved that I had waited too long.

It was always unnerving to lose something over the side, not necessarily because it was a thing of value, but because it was a reminder of how quickly it could happen to a person (meaning oneself) and how irredeemable such an accident would be. From time to time I would throw an empty tin over the side and watch it vanish behind, just to remind me to hold on tight when working on the foredeck.

In the dense fog and cold, I stayed below as much as possible, huddling around the heater like a road mender at his brazier. I would thaw my hands, then swivel around to scorch my feet and socks until they had stopped steaming. But I did not like to leave the heater on when I was asleep and unable to watch it, so I relied on two sleeping bags and my faithful hot-water bottle to keep me warm at night. Even so, I always felt cold, mainly as a result of my hourly excursions on deck. My body clock seemed to turn off my interior heating system at night and I shivered violently as soon as I got up. By the time I returned to my bunk, my teeth were rattling like castanets and I was shaking. It took several minutes to warm up again and fall asleep.

The loneliness of that ocean made me anxious for human company and I looked forward to making my radio calls with even greater anticipation than usual. I spoke to Jacques at the farm in the evenings and to Jack Hill every other day. And the news they gave me was very exciting. Alain Colas in *Club Méditerranée* had put into St. Johns, Newfoundland, for repairs and was expected to leave shortly, while the great Eric Tabarly in *Pen Duick VI* was approaching Newport. I was delighted to hear Tabarly was doing so well. He was a fine seaman, and the most quiet and unassuming of men who was greatly respected by everyone. He had won the race 12 years before, in the 44-foot *Pen Duick II*. The present *Pen Duick* was a 73-foot racing machine designed to be sailed by 12 men, and how he managed that vessel alone no one knew. But then he was a remarkable man. *Club Med,* on the other hand, had been designed for one man. But even with all the modern labor-saving gadgets it was impossible to manage such a massive boat effectively when singlehanded and I was not surprised to hear that Colas was lagging behind.

Although Tabarly was approaching Newport, I was sure the first boat to arrive would be *Three Cheers*. Mike had been confident he could do the crossing in 18 days and, since that was only one day away, I expected to hear news of his arrival very soon.

129

To keep myself company in the evenings I quite often listened to the BBC Overseas Service. The programs were a marvelous mixture of news, education, and items on obscure topics like "Hedge Trimming in Britain Today." They also broadcast fascinating plays with characters called Rodney, Cynthia, and Charles, who played polo when they weren't murdering each other. Sometimes I left the radio on without really listening to it because it was so nice to hear human voices.

One item of news that had me gasping was the announcement that the weather in Britain was the hottest since they knew not when. Temperatures of 90 degrees plus were being recorded, cattle were being given sunshades, and most of London seemed to be jumping into the fountains at Trafalgar Square. I went up into the cockpit and had a look around; obviously I was on a different planet, probably Mars. It was very odd to be freezing on a latitude 300 miles to the south of Plymouth.

Astonishingly, on the morning of my seventeenth day at sea, the sun suddenly appeared through the fog and burned most of it away. The horizon was still hidden in mist, so I didn't get too excited about fixing my position. But then it too became visible and I rushed into action with sextant and chronometer. Yet I was very puzzled at the results. They made no sense in relation to my dead-reckoning position. I checked the workings, but could find no error there, so I took more sun sights. But the results were the same. It appeared I was over the Flemish Cap, a bank 90 miles to the east of the Grand Banks themselves. And I thought I had passed to the south of that bank hours before. I was pretty disgusted with my navigation. It was one thing to be out on my latitude, which I had estimated from my course sailed (a very difficult thing to judge accurately), but to be badly out on my longitude as well? I had estimated this from my distance run, normally quite a good measure, but I must have been miles out somewhere — and I didn't even know where.

A nagging suspicion remained and I checked the sextant

for error, but there was nothing out of the ordinary. I tried to check the chronometer as well, but could pick up no radio time signals at that time of day. Much later I heard a Greenwich Time Signal on the BBC and glanced automatically at the chronometer. I could hardly believe my eyes — it was not just seconds slow, it was minutes slow. For every second that the chronometer was out, there would be an error of one mile in my navigation. This timepiece had been reasonably accurate for most of the trip, losing a steady one second a week, but now it had suddenly lost hundreds of seconds. The trouble was, I had no way of knowing exactly how slow it had been when I took the sights, so I could not rework my calculations. As a result, yet again, I had no firm idea of my position. And by this time the fog had come down again, so there was no chance of taking fresh sights. The best I could do was to work up my dead reckoning again.

After throwing a few appropriate remarks in the direction of the chronometer, which I had bought at considerable expense just before the race, I started going back over my chartwork. After making a best estimate of my position, I also plotted positions that allowed for all the likely errors and unknowns that could have crept in and drew a circle around the lot. All I could say was that I was probably somewhere in that circle and it was a large circle at that. In the middle of the ocean such vagueness wouldn't have mattered, but here I had the unpleasant feeling it might, for I was approaching iceberg country.

Not that I was too worried about icebergs. There were so few of them about that year, and the ten or 20 that had been reported had drifted off to the south and east of me. Admittedly there were more on their way down from the north, but at the point where I was likely to meet them, they were in a path that ran down the eastern edge of the banks from north to south. This path was perhaps 60 miles wide, but compared to the way the bergs spread out farther south, this really seemed quite narrow when you were dashing across it with your eyes closed. A mere half-day's sail. I only wished I could be sure that I was approaching this narrow section. My circle seemed to touch an awful lot of places where from my study of the *Pilot*, I was quite certain there were clusters of enormous bergs lying in wait.

Ridiculous to worry about it, I decided. Only a few icebergs. Thousands of square miles of ocean. Can't do much about it anyway. So, after a delicious supper of tomatoes and cheese on toast, and an hour listening to Brahms, I gave a last shiver and went to sleep.

The wind was up and down during the night and I had to make a couple of difficult sail changes that lost me a lot of sleep. At dawn I took a look on deck, my eyes opening out of habit rather than desire, and at the sight of the usual white blanket, staggered back to my bunk for some more vivid dreams. An hour later I awoke but did not bother to go up on deck, merely checking the compass and swiveling my little black box in a circle. I could see that the fog was still about and I could sense that the boat was going well, so there didn't seem any point in getting cold on deck. When I next awoke I was surprised to find I had overslept and hurried up on deck, my eyes blinking from the light. To my delight I found the fog had cleared and I could see as far as the horizon ahead. This was a nice surprise!

Then I looked behind.

At first my eyes didn't comprehend. There was so much dazzling whiteness, the craggy mountains were so brilliant in the morning light that they seemed to be part of the sky. But white they were and craggy too. Two large icebergs a mile astern. One probably a quarter of a mile long, flat and rectangular. The other very tall with a sharp point at one end. And then my eye caught a third, gray with shadow and jagged too.

I whimpered slightly and sat down before my knees did it for me. The *Golly* was as steady as a rock in the light wind and, guided by the indefatigable self-steering, was holding a perfect course. I knew that by her wake, which was as straight as a ruler. Following the course of that straight line I could see exactly where we had been a few minutes before. And that was between the two large bergs.

I am not a very religious person; at one point I was actually a nonbeliever, but there are times when one doesn't make an issue of these things. And I said a heartfelt prayer to the effect that if there was Someone Up There, I was really terribly grateful for the icebergs having been moved out of my path or for me having been moved out of theirs, whichever was the case. And, although I didn't merit it, and was very ungrateful, and absolutely the least deserving, would God awfully mind keeping an eye on me just a little bit longer? I obviously needed the assistance.

I sat looking at the bergs for half an hour, until they began to disappear over the horizon. I couldn't stop thinking about one thing. I must have passed within yards of those bergs, and if I'd been on a fractionally different course, I would have hit one. My sixth sense had really let me down — but then it had always functioned best in response to cruise liners with their hot baths and five-course dinners.

Like someone delivered from the jaws of a lion, I thereafter decided that life was really quite wonderful. Winching in genoas became a positive and uplifting experience, particularly for my biceps, and the chores became just another part of the rich pageant of life. As if to purify my soul and make me feel that I had deserved my escape, I rushed around the boat cleaning, dusting, oiling, and rubbing. I took eight sun sights during the day, using the ordinary cabin clock, which I checked for accuracy at least ten times. I scrubbed the galley. I put a hand into the depth of the food lockers, a brave venture, because it was not unusual to have damp and moldy spaghetti coil itself around one's fingers. I bagged some sails lying loose in the sailbin. And of course I did the washing up.

Then the wind died. It seemed a good time to have a belated celebration and I had a very small glass of Scotch, which was delightful. There was only one thing missing and that was some human company, so I called my parents and had a chat. It was such a relief to talk to someone, and I was so full of things to talk about, that I twittered on endlessly. It was the last talk I would have with my parents before they flew to New York two days later.

But it was taking longer and longer to get through on the radio. The distance to Portishead was now nearly 2,000 miles and I found it increasingly difficult to be heard above the commercial shipping. Once Portishead had picked up my call there was no problem. They would tune their antennae to my position and hear me quite well. But that initial call was agony. After waiting through perhaps three calls lasting 15 minutes each, I would try to make contact during a pause and find several vessels talking over me. Sometimes the operator would keep listening for other people who wanted to speak, but other times he wouldn't wait, and I would almost weep with frustration as I heard him starting to connect a long queue of calls. As time went on I was less able to cope with these disappointments. Tiredness and general wear and tear had made me fretful and short-tempered. Even the elation of having escaped the iceberg lasted only a day and was soon replaced by the tiredness and lassitude I had felt before.

I had the Three-Quarter Way Stage to look forward to, just two days ahead if I kept to my average speed. I was passing over the Grand Banks, about 120 miles to the south of Cape Race, and aiming to pass 30 miles to the south of Sable Island. But it was slow progress. The wind was light and for the most part from ahead. Whichever tack I chose, it appeared to be the unfavorable one, and I was constantly tacking to try to improve my heading. The weather forecast predicted a northwesterly wind, which would have been ideal, but it never materialized and I settled down to make the best of what little westerly wind there was.

The lack of good progress was disappointing but not entirely unexpected after the good run I had experienced so far, and I was more concerned with the possibility of meeting one of the fishing fleets often found in the area. The Russians had particularly large fleets and competitors in previous races had bumped into more than one of their ships before now. It is well known that fishermen never get out of anyone's way, and they are singularly unimpressed by sailing yachts. Even if they saw a small vessel approaching in thick fog on their radar, I had doubts as to whether they would do anything. But then my feelings about fishermen had been colored by one in the Channel who had altered course directly across my bows and watched in delight as I had jibed in a confusion of sheets and backed sails. Doubtless they had a poor opinion of yachtsmen too.

I kept a particularly good lookout for the next two days, and when it was foggy I used the radar detector continuously. I didn't want to be sunk and picked up by a Russian in case his next port of call was Omsk.

Keeping a good watch and constantly retrimming the sails in the light wind had me on deck busy much of the time. I managed to sleep even less than before. My daily average was about six hours, but for two days I had only four, which soon affected my morale and my judgment. I overslept at the wrong times and then couldn't get to sleep when I had the opportunity. When I was really dropping with fatigue, the wind would be at its most demanding, constantly changing direction and strength. I would tweak the self-steering control line to put the *Golly* back on course, retrim the sails, wait for her to settle down, and then find she was off course again. Possibly it wasn't worth all the bother — some of the time we were only going at one knot. But I got a great deal of satisfaction from making that one knot in hardly more than a whisper of wind and the effort seemed worthwhile.

Thunder and torrential rain drifted in from the west, but the atmosphere was sultry and promised no steady breeze. Great black clouds hung low overhead, apparently stationary in the sky, and the air was as heavy as lead. It was almost impossible to receive any radio transmissions with so much electricity in the air, but I managed to hear a weather forecast from Canso in Nova Scotia. It predicted variable winds turning easterly. If it were true, then it would be nice to have a downhill run after so many westerlies.

In the evening a breeze came up from the northwest, cleared the fog away, and veered steadily around to the east. How delightful it was to be reaching, then running before the wind! I put up the spinnaker and the *Golly* ticked off at a steady four knots. With the wind still veering I had to jibe the spinnaker, not one of my favorite tasks, but it was reasonably safe with the "salami" to slide down over the sail while I rearranged booms, sheets, and guys for the new jibe. Half an hour later I had to jibe again as the wind shifted back 30 degrees, but at last she seemed to be settled on course, traveling at five knots as the wind freshened.

It had been a long day and my eyelids were falling shut whenever they chose. For a split second I even fell asleep on my feet and, taking the hint, I went below for a well-earned rest. My bunk seemed even more welcoming than usual that night. The temperature was much warmer now, so that I didn't have to defrost myself before falling asleep. And I had the prospect of a good hour's rest without having to get up and trim a single sail.

As I fell into my bunk I hardly gave a thought to what the wind might be doing next. All I cared about was sleep in large quantities and preferably unadorned by dreams of icebergs.

136

10

As I awoke I became aware that something was wrong. The boat was moving wildly, rolling from side to side then suddenly lurching over and staying there, shuddering with strain. With a groan I remembered the spinnaker. By the feel of the boat, it should have been down hours ago. Still dazed and heavy-eyed, I could not think how long I had been asleep, but it must have been well over an hour, probably nearer two. I pulled on my boots and oilskins and staggered up on deck, nervous of what I might find.

It could have been worse. The wind was Force 5 and still from the east. The seas were not any larger than I would have expected, but they were sufficient to make the boat roll considerably and slue from side to side. It was impossible for the self-steering to anticipate these yaws until too late, and only when the boat was well off track could the wind vane sense it and pull her back. But the pull of the spinnaker was often too powerful and the *Golly* would continue to veer off until the spinnaker held her over on her side, lee rail under and main boom dragging in the water. These broaches were horrible to see. They put a lot of strain on the boat, particularly the mast and rigging, and I hurried to lower the spinnaker before she broached again.

Lowering a spinnaker in a strong breeze when alone at night was a frightening experience. One mistake and the spinnaker could tear and wrap itself around the forestay, making it impossible to raise a foresail again. The spinnaker boom, the guy and sheet, were all under enormous strain and one slip could result in serious breakage. I wasn't going to take any chances and approached the task with caution. Better to be slow and sure than make a mistake.

The "salami" would not slide down over a full spinnaker, so I had to half-collapse the sail before attempting to pull the sausage down over it. Having eased the sheet, there was a terrible commotion of flapping canvas and rattling gear as I rushed forward to pull the sleeve down. I tugged on the line, but nothing happened. I pulled harder, but the mouth of the "salami" stayed obstinately where it was, at the top of the sail. At that moment the *Golly* broached and I had to cling on as she dived around on her side. For a moment all was confusion, then she righted herself and thundered off into the night. I yanked on the line again, but I could make no impression on the "salami" at all. A fine time to jam itself. I tried collapsing the spinnaker farther, but after a terrifying broach I decided that, whatever the method, the important thing was to get the spinnaker down quickly.

The traditional method of lowering a spinnaker is most satisfactory if you have a crew of five or ten, but singlehanded it requires five arms and, with my method, three feet. Having let one corner of the sail fly, you pull on the other corner, gather in the foot of the sail (quite impossible), then with your arms full of sail you let off the halyard. This was where the feet came in. I wrapped them around the sail in place of arms. The halyard must then be lowered slowly. This was where the third foot was needed. I put the halyard under my foot, let it run out a way, then stopped it by stamping hard. Except I sometimes missed, or found my leg in the air with the halyard wrapped around my foot and pulling hard. As the sail came down, all was meant to be gathered in tidily, and in no time the spinnaker should be lying at one's feet in a neat pile.

This time I dropped half the thing in the water, and twice nearly took off behind the ballooning sail. But it was down, and I breathed a sigh of relief. Half an hour later I had sorted out the mess of lines, booms, guys, and sheets, and hoisted a jib boomed out to windward.

Sleep. That was all and everything I had ever wanted, and I shot below to fall into a heavy and dreamless slumber.

Dutifully I heard the alarm an hour later and crawled out of my bunk. The wind had increased, and the boat was running too fast again so that I lowered the jib and left her under mainsail only. This was lazy of me. I should have reefed the main and put up a smaller jib, but I couldn't face the effort and hurried back to my bunk instead.

At three in the morning (everything at sea happens at three in the morning), I awoke with that familiar feeling that something was wrong again. I was thick with sleep and longing to snuggle into the depths of my sleeping bag, but I managed to pull myself up and take a look on deck. I was shocked to find it was blowing a gale and the boat was careering downhill, veering from side to side as the large waves caught her from behind. Then I did something extraordinary. I must have been half asleep with my brain even more addled than usual. Nothing else could explain the stupidity of my actions.

I decided I must reef the main immediately. Usually, even in the worst crises, I can amaze myself by taking a calm look at the situation and setting about everything in a careful way. But this time I rushed into action, without thought and without consideration of the consequences. I decided I must get the *Golly* up into the wind to reef the main, and straightaway. Mustn't strain the self-steering, I thought. Mustn't use it to bring her up. It'll be too sudden for it.

This was completely backward thinking. I knew very well that the self-steering was all right as long as it was in use, but that once it was disconnected it was free to swing too far and destroy itself. But somehow my brain had decided that the exact opposite was true and I was determined to unlatch the gear.

Perhaps it was also fear from the terrible rushing downward, that violent swerving from side to side that made me panic. It was unnerving to be rocketing into the darkness, more or less out of control. But whatever it was, tiredness or fear, I did it. I unlatched the gear and pushed the tiller hard over so that the *Golly* would shoot up into the wind and allow me to reef. As the boat turned, the self-steering was thrust sideways. Then, as she fell back again, the gear was pushed the other way. Instinctively I looked back at the gear and my heart froze. All four of the metal struts were bent out of recognition.

The full idiocy of what I had done hit me like a sledgehammer. It was such an obvious and basic mistake, and so irredeemable. I groaned and muttered, "Oh, you twit!" which was quite kind under the circumstances, and drew a breath.

It was difficult to decide how serious my situation really was. One moment I would look at the twisted arms and despair, and the next I would feel a sudden hope that I could once again repair them. The implications of failure were unpleasant — a long trek up to Nova Scotia without self-steering — so I knew I must at least try to straighten those arms. I lowered the mainsail and had a close look at the gear. It would be impossibly difficult to mend the gear in position, so I decided I would have to bring the lower section of the gear inboard where I could dismantle it with greater ease. The only problem was the weight and size of the gear. Made of a heavy alloy, and more than five feet in height, it weighed about 140 pounds to my 98.

Gathering the necessary tools around me, I started the long and tedious task. I disconnected the various ropes and lines attached to the gear, leaving one line firmly secured to both the gear and the boat. Even allowing for my depleted brain power, I could see it wouldn't be a good idea to drop the gear over the side. Next I had to slide the main spindle out. The whole of the lower moving section of the gear swung on this main spindle, a stainless-steel rod an inch thick. Once it was removed the section would be completely unsupported and would drop into the water, whereupon I would pull it up over the rail, hopefully. But I found the removal of the spindle was not just a matter of sliding it out. The gear had to be held up in position while I worked the spindle out, inch by inch. As before I was leaning over the stern rail, gripping with my feet, and often up to my elbows in water. But now I was trying to hold a weight in a precise position while tugging at a spindle as well.

Finally, after much effort, the spindle came away and I felt the lower section of the gear fall as I tried to take its weight. I held on grimly, resting a moment while I waited for a suitable wave that would help me swing the gear around and up over the rail. Without the buoyancy of the water I could never have swung the gear, let alone held it. At last I felt the stern rising and saw the surface rushing up as a large wave approached. I swung the gear around and heaved. But I didn't quite make it the first time and, with a gasp, I had to let the gear fall into the water again. By this time my arms were very tired and I had to take a long rest before attempting the lift again. I hung over the stern, holding firmly on to that precious metal, and waited for perhaps half a minute. A large wave came, I heaved and got the gear halfway onto the rail. But the weight was still on the wrong side and I felt it slipping back. Summoning some strength I gave a last pull and managed to slide it over another inch. At last, by swinging my weight on it, the gear pivoted over onto my side of the rail. Then, after a final heave, it fell on top of me. I lay back on the wet deck, exhausted but very relieved.

I lay there for five minutes or so, enjoying the rest. I was not in any hurry to get on with the repairs. They would take a long time at whatever speed I tackled them, so I might as well take them slowly and thoughtfully — unlike my earlier actions. Every moment that the *Golly* lay there drifting, we were forfeiting mileage. Seven or eight knots was the *Golly's* speed downwind in a good breeze. It was sad to lose such easy progress, but it was more important to get the gear repaired properly than to rush the job and bend the gear again.

Leaving the *Golly* drifting, I dismantled the bent struts and took them below for that favorite task of mine — weld-bending, as I called it. After heating the struts I attempted to bend them. But either the blow lamp and the gas rings never got the struts hot enough or else the metal wasn't heatable anyway, because the heat never seemed to make much difference. So in the end it was always back to plain old bending. The main problem was finding some leverage against which to bend the metal. Most of the interior fittings were wood and too soft to form a good base for the vise, so that the boat echoed to the sound of splintering wood as I tried the vise on bulkheads, bunk ends, and shelf edges. By the time I had got the worst bends out, the interior of·the boat looked like matchwood.

It took me five hours of sweat and toil to straighten the struts and even then they looked like snakes. As before, I hung on them, swung on them, heaved, pushed, and yanked. Sometimes I would even make the kinks worse by exerting the pressure in the wrong place, but I only did that five times, then I learned. Quick, I am.

I also discovered that I was brainless, for the tenth time that day. As I grunted and pulled and heaved I suddenly realized that I had wasted five whole hours in useless pursuit, trying to bend metal against wood. There had been the perfect leverage available all the time. I had been so intent on using the vise I had forgotten it would be completely unnecessary if I levered the struts directly against the most solid and well-bedded metal you could find: the engine. It took me ten minutes to straighten all four struts against the engine, and the thought of five hours' wasted effort almost made me laugh or weep, I wasn't sure which. I gave up self-reproach and crawled on deck to reassemble the gear.

It was still blowing a gale from the east, very gray but mercifully warmer than before so that I could work without freezing hands and after half an hour the gear was ready to put back over the side. But I decided to wait. I was worried about the main casting, which had been cracked during the storm (was it months before?). The main casting supported the spindle at either end and would be under severe strain as I slid the spindle back into position. It would only need one wave to twist the lower section around and the casting would surely break.

I decided to wait until the gale abated. But rather than waste more of that following wind, I set a small jib and steered by hand for a while. But I was dog tired and it was all I could do to keep awake for more than a moment. Technicolor dreams leaped into my head at every opportunity and wild situations rushed through my imagination like a horrendous carnival.

Eventually I decided the wind had abated sufficiently to put the self-steering back on. This was a lot of nonsense. The waves were just as large as before, but my judgment had gone and, in my eagerness to get the gear working again, so that I could sleep, I was not as cautious as I should have been.

If the effort of taking the gear off was tiring, it was terrible to put it back. Once I had swung it over the rail I had to hold it in a precise position so that I could slide the spindle in through the holes in the casting and the lower section. The gear was turning and twisting with every movement of the boat and the waves and, with only one hand free to hold it, it was an impossible weight to maneuver. With my other hand, I just managed to get the spindle in through one end of the main casting and part of the lower section when I felt something give. Then the whole of the lower section was swinging sideways and with a sinking heart I saw why. The main casting had sheared. It hung in two sections, split across the middle and completely unable to do its job of supporting the spindle and the gear. With a last superhuman effort I hoisted the lower section inboard and sat down to rest.

Whichever way I looked at it, I could not go on without self-steering. And without a welding kit complete with masked welder I could see no way of repairing the gear. What an idiot I'd been — so impatient to get going that I'd broken the gear beyond repair. I flung reproaches and recriminations at myself, but it didn't do any good. I was still faced with the problem of what to do next. And it always came back to two alternatives. Mend the gear or make for the nearest port.

I looked at the gear from every angle. I wondered how I might support it, but I could think of nothing that would be strong enough to hold the casting solid against the considerable strains it must withstand. There seemed to be no hope and yet I couldn't believe it. There must be a fiendishly clever way of fixing that gear, but my slender knowledge of metallurgy, carpentry, not to mention engineering did not volunteer a single solution.

I was miserable, but there was nothing for it but to examine the chart and look for a suitable port. And, as I reminded myself, it could be a great deal worse. This might have happened in the middle of the empty stretch between Newfoundland and England and then I would have had a much greater problem. As it was, Newfoundland was 140 miles to the north, while Nova Scotia was more than 200 miles to the northwest. Although it was farther, I much preferred Nova Scotia because it was closer to my route. With a bit of luck I could get there in two or three days and, allowing a day for repairs, I would lose a total of only three to four days. The rules of the race permitted competitors to stop at any port they wished, so I could continue to race as before.

It was difficult to know which port to make for. I had a large chart of Nova Scotia, but there appeared to be no major harbors on the coast except for Halifax, which was miles away. The nearest small harbor was Canso, on the eastern tip of the land. It had a radio beacon to guide me in, and a radio station from which I had received weather forecasts. If it was large enough to have a radio station it should be large enough for me, or that's what I thought anyway.

My first instinct was to call England and let them know what had happened. My parents were in the States, Jacques would be at work, so I tried Jack Hill. But, for all the times I had got through, this was the one occasion when it was impossible. Greeks were exchanging news on everyone in the village, Italians were talking to each one of their 15 children, and a chap from Liverpool wanted to know why his wife hadn't been in when he phoned last Saturday night (she'd been at her Mum's, she said).

It was frustrating to sit there by the radio, longing to talk to someone, but utterly helpless to get through. I decided to try Canso instead, and was greatly cheered when they answered straightaway. After explaining my problems, I asked for information on Canso Harbor and its suitability for me; whether it was easy to enter, whether it had welding facilities, and so on. The radio operator asked me to wait while he found out. (Didn't he know about the size of the harbor, at least?) He came back and asked me how much my vessel drew. I replied six feet. Ohhh, he replied, he didn't know about that. (If it didn't have six feet of water, then what did it have? Rocks?) I kept asking for details; was it well buoyed, was there a pilot, did the pilot vessel have radar to find me in the fog? Considering the radio station was also a coast guard station, they were horribly vague. Eventually I was told there was a pilot, but that was about all they could tell me.

I felt more miserable than before. Here I was faced with three days at the tiller, little sleep, and at the end of it a harbor that might not be a harbor at all. And it was bound to be shrouded in fog, whatever it was. Nevertheless I decided to make for Canso and try to get more information as I approached. I calculated my course as 300 degrees and climbed wearily up into the cockpit to start the long and tedious tack of hand steering for over 200 miles.

Tiredness can be a pleasant feeling when sleep is imminent, but I was now exhausted, and if I wanted to reach land in a few days, I would have to cut my sleep down to the very minimum. I had been very tired the day before but now, after a night and morning of heaving the self-steering about, I was in a zombielike daze. I found myself staring at the compass but not reading it. Then I would fall asleep for seconds at a time, my head on my chest until the boat would slew off course and the motion wake me. The gale had abated, but there were still big seas running so I had to steer carefully. But twice I fell asleep at the wrong moment and awoke to find myself up to my waist in water as a wave swept into the cockpit. The water soon drained away, but I was left wet and cold, although I hardly noticed it.

I steered on and on for hours in a nightmare of half-sleep and grim, gray reality. Most of the time I hardly knew what I was doing, yet I was aware of one thing. I must press on; I must get to Newport somehow, or else my family would have left. That thought drove me on with grim determination through those endless hours.

At last by the late evening, the sea dropped to manageable proportions. There was no danger of being pooped again. And, with a bit of luck, there was hope of persuading the *Golly* to steer herself by careful balancing and trimming of the sails. I experimented with different sail areas and finally settled on a reefed main and working jib. Although this left the *Golly* very much underpowered, she did stay more or less on course for up to ten minutes at a time. This gave me a chance to do other things. First I looked at the chart and tried to estimate our position. At the same time I checked the course, 300 degrees. Then I groaned and buried my head in my hands. Just to compound my series of mistakes, I had been steering 330 degrees for the last seven hours, not 300 degrees. In my exhausted state this was almost too much to bear and, after all that I had been through, after the hours of effort and toil, it was the straw that broke my back. I sat down and wept great floods of tears.

After a while I sat back and reached for the bottle of whiskey. I don't drink at sea, but this didn't count because it was strictly medicinal. After a couple of drams I began to feel better. After three, life began picking up. And the fourth had me thinking about parties and human company and it being Saturday evening. I wanted to talk to someone more than ever and, knowing that Jacques had gone to see his family in Paris, I tried to call Jack Hill again. This time I got through straightaway. It was midnight in England and Jack had been asleep, but I would never have known it from his cheerful response. But he was very upset at my news, particularly when I told him the gear was unrepairable. He offered to go and fetch Jacques from on board *Gulliver G* to give me advice, but I pointed out that he wouldn't be there. But Jacques, said Jack, had never gone to Paris!

I had good reason to be very grateful to Jack Hill that night. Not only did he insist that I speak to Jacques straight-away, but he sprinted across Lymington, picked Jacques up from the boat, and had him by the phone in half an hour. Although Jacques was a wizard with mechanical things, I didn't hold out much hope of his finding a solution. But he was adamant. "You can't get to Nova Scotia without some self-steering," he repeated several times. "Put lashing on it, string it together, anything so that you can sleep!" I felt a small ray of hope and, after arranging to call again 12 hours later, set to work on the lashing.

The casting had a jagged break in it and when the two pieces were pressed together, they fitted like a jigsaw. That little ray of hope became brighter; if I could lash the two pieces together firmly enough, the jaggedness would hold the casting in place, preventing sideways movement. But I would have to get the lashing really tight and I could never do that by pulling alone. I considered a kind of tourniquet, but settled on double lashings, one around the casting and another to pull on the first one at right angles, like a bowman pulling on the string of his bow.

I placed lashings at every conceivable angle and tightened

them time and time again until the casting was held in a viselike grip. By this time I was certain it would work. What a simple solution it was. If I had thought of it when the casting had only been cracked, it would never have broken. But thanks to Jacques's practical mind I had the solution now before I lost any more time.

All I had to do now was lift the lower section of the gear into place. It should have been easier in the calmer seas, but I soon found it wasn't. Without the buoyancy of the large waves the gear felt like a ton weight as I lifted it over the side. With the spindle between my teeth, I maneuvered it into position and, holding it there with one hand, grabbed the spindle with the other and tried to slide it in. Twice I had to stop and rest, letting the gear fall into the water until I had the strength to lift it again. But at last I felt the spindle slide in through one hole, another, and finally all four. Another rest, and I was ready to connect the various lines and pulleys.

Not only was the gear back together again, but it worked. And, though I watched the casting like a hawk, it never moved an inch. I felt as though a massive weight had been lifted from my mind. What a marvelous turnabout in my luck. I was on my way under self-steering again, and able to sleep. Leaving the *Golly* on course for Nova Scotia, I fell into my bunk and slept a dreamless sleep.

The next day I awoke a new person, still tired but no longer exhausted. My body felt as if it had been through three rounds with a wrestler, and an angry one at that. I was very still and ached all over, so that every movement brought a twinge from complaining muscles. Nevertheless, I felt marvelous.

I looked at the self-steering as I had done at intervals through the night. The struts were straight, if you ignored the slight kinks and the casting was meshed firmly together. But there was one small thing bothering me. I was still heading for Canso. This was the sensible thing to do, for the gear must be permanently repaired if it was to survive another gale. And yet I longed to turn for Newport. I worked out that a stop in Canso would put my arrival back to the seventh or eighth of July at the very best. I didn't care about the race. I had already lost well over two days and was sure that I must be miles behind everyone else, but I did care about seeing Jacques and my parents for more than just a couple of days.

There was no more doubt in my mind. I turned the *Golly* around and headed for Newport.

After that my spirits soared. I called the two J's in Lymington and they were absolutely delighted to hear that I was heading for Newport. But, in his usual thoughtful way, the wonderful Jack Hill had found charts of Canso and every other harbor along the coast in case I should need information about them. Jack was a marvelous ally. Out of curiosity I asked Jacques what Canso looked like on the large chart. "Er . . . interesting," he said.

"That bad, eh?"

"Er . . . yes."

Which meant it must be surrounded by rocks, full of shoals, and exposed to the seas. I was rather glad I wasn't going there.

The next 24 hours were blissful. I slept nearly all the time, just pausing to put food in my mouth, check the sails, and eye the self-steering. I even found out where I was. My position was disappointing, of course. After struggling to make all that southing, I had rushed north and was just where I had planned not to be. I would now pass to the north of Sable Island where there was more likelihood of being becalmed, and certainly more chance of meeting fishing boats. But it would not be worth working around to the south of the island again, so I pressed on hoping to gain some southing later.

Sable Island is a graveyard of ships. Long, low and, like everything else in the area, often hidden in fog, it forms a natural trap. But I soon picked up its radio beacon and by taking numerous bearings on it, I was confident I was well clear of it. Now all I had to worry about were boats and the self-steering.

After a day of sunshine and breezes, the mist came down

and the wind dropped. On went my little black box to listen for fishing boats and up went more sail. But I was still being very careful about straining the self-steering. I was determined not to put up too much canvas, go too fast and ruin the gear yet again. Caution and care were the most important considerations, not speed. With a light easterly wind I would have hoisted a spinnaker under normal circumstances, but it would not be wise now. Anyway, I was looking forward to another long sleep and a spinnaker would be too much like hard work.

Then I saw it: a yacht clearly visible through the fog. It had to be one of us, but who? I got out the binoculars and peered. The boat seemed to be smaller than the *Golly*, white-hulled and, I was somewhat peeved to notice, carrying a spinnaker! I thought I recognized the boat and yet I couldn't quite place her. Nor could I identify her number at first; it was just too far away to see. But I kept peering through the glasses, and finally managed to pick out a number, then another, and hurried below to look her up. It was that new racing stripe down the side that had fooled me. It hadn't been there during the Round Britain Race. But there was no doubt it was Gustaf, the cuddly Belgian, in the *Golly's* smaller sister, *Tyfoon*. I switched on the VHF, gave him a call, and we were soon chattering away like squirrels.

"We haf bottle of champagne in Newport, yes?" said Gustaf.

"Absolutely," I replied.

"Vot about two?"

"Even better."

"Last von to arrive gifs first bottle, yes?"

"You drive a hard bargain, Gustaf, but you're on."

There was not a moment to lose and, scuttling around like an ant, I had the spinnaker hoisted and pulling within minutes. If the self-steering fell apart it was just too bad. Never mind all this careful and safe progress at the expense of speed. It was Newport or bust!

11

I may have wanted to make all speed again, but the wind had other ideas. As I left Sable Island to the south and ran parallel to the Nova Scotia coast, heading for Nantucket Island and the turning point for Newport, the wind remained light and fluky with the promise of a flat calm at any moment. There was fog of course. It was a thinner, warmer fog than before, but very much more persistent and I was not able to take a sun sight for five days, the longest I had ever gone without a fix. But I could get a fairly good idea of my position from the excellent system of radio beacons that line the Nova Scotia coast, and from soundings.

As before, I found that I was being pushed due west instead of south of west, the course I was aiming for. If I had passed to the south of Sable Island, this would not have mattered so much, but I found myself getting closer and closer to the coast and, like most sailors, I didn't like it one bit. I tacked away several times, but seemed to be pulled back like a magnet. I was actually never closer than 20 miles, but in that fog it felt uncomfortably near.

I heard fishing boats' engines and picked up their radar several times, but they never came close, and once clear of the land, they seemed to vanish altogether.

Although the fog was persistent, the misty air was at least warm. Since leaving the Grand Banks the temperature had leaped up and I was able to cease being a bear. With two layers of clothing removed, my arms stopped sticking out sideways and I could move them quite easily. One sleeping bag became sufficient to keep me warm at night, although I did continue to take a hot-water bottle to bed with me because in anything less than the tropics, my feet are small and unmelting blocks of ice. I would have preferred bright sunlight to go with the warmth, particularly when I looked at my unattractively pallid and anemic skin, which bore no resemblance to the suntanned supergirl I had hoped to be. But I was not complaining. The important thing to remember was that life could always be worse — I might find myself back on the Grand Banks or working in an office again.

On the twenty-ninth of June, Jack Hill told me that Tabarly had won the Pen Duick Trophy in 23 days 20 hours after having been becalmed off Newport for four days. He had lost his self-steering gear in one of the early gales and continued without it. This was a feat of seamanship that only Tabarly could have pulled off. I was delighted to hear that he had won, although I was disappointed at the same time. *Three Cheers* should have been able to beat *Pen Duick* easily, and I was sad to hear that Mike had not squeaked in first.

Having lost at least two days and probably three as a result of my self-steering troubles, I was still four or five days from Newport. However the Fourth of July was also five days away, so I wasn't too unhappy about the lost time. With a bit of luck I might yet arrive in time for the celebrations, although I wasn't counting on it. That would be asking for trouble. However I did let thoughts of Newport begin to enter my mind. Hot bath, food, bed, in that order, followed shortly by lots more of the same. As the days passed my imaginings became more specific. The bath would be up to

152

my chin and so hot I could hardly bear it. As I lay there, a glass of cool white wine would magically appear and the scent of cooking food would drift in. Lunch would be unbelievably delicious, mainly because it would have been prepared by someone else. And finally, the thing I had been waiting for all my life — sleep. Long, uninterrupted by dreams, and absolutely alarmless.

In the meantime I had to get to Newport. This was as much hard work as ever. The wind was up and down and always varying in direction, which meant sail changing. But with the end in sight I developed a kind of gritty determination that had me hoisting and winching with new resolution. If the sails tried to blow over the side I growled at them, if they dared to balloon I leaped on them from a great height, and if they stuck going down the forehatch I stood on them until the sails suddenly shot down into the bin with me close behind. I dealt with my *bête noir*, the Number One genoa, in a new no-nonsense way. As I pulled it up from the sailbin section by section and it got stuck as it always did, I gave up the subtle approach and the looking to see what the problem was that never got me anywhere. Instead I just braced my feet and pulled harder, roaring and grunting like an elephant. Once, so gritty was my determination that the sail suddenly shot out and sent me sliding backward across the deck. My progress was stopped by a cleat on the backbone that made me speechless with pain and unable to utter my second very rude word of my trip.

After a week spent with friends near New York, my parents should have arrived in Newport by this time, and I decided to call them through Halifax the next morning. I was put through in five minutes and heard my parents as clearly as if they were just yards away. They had plenty of news for me. *Club Méditerranée* had arrived second without sinking anything en route. And the third boat to finish and win the Jester Trophy was, incredibly, a tiny 30-foot catamaran called *The Third Turtle* sailed by Mike Birch. This was the most amazing achievement and a great triumph for a small

boat. But the news that stopped me in my tracks was the news of the fourth boat to finish. It was my Polish friend *Spaniel*. For the first time I realized how well I must have been doing until the disaster of the self-steering. Later when I checked *Spaniel'*s positions against mine I found he had been a hundred miles ahead of me over the Grand Banks — that is, about one day's sailing. But the day after my self-steering broke (while I was still hove to), his lead had leaped to 200 miles. Races are full of ifs and buts, but I couldn't help thinking that if I had managed to stay close behind him I might have been finishing that very day.

Ideas of what might have been were forgotten as Mother gave me some new thoughts on the suitability of my Atlantic wardrobe.

"Now, darling, about all this terrible cold," said Mother anxiously. "I didn't realize it was going to be freezing. Are you wrapping up well?"

"Oh, don't worry," I replied. "It's much warmer now."

"But are you likely to meet more icebergs?" she asked. "In which case you really *should* be well dressed."

As I pondered this suggestion, Mother suddenly declared, "By the way, there's going to be an amazing welcome for you!" There was a pause while thoughts of ticker tape and brass bands fluttered through my mind to be instantly rejected in favor of Mother and Father brandishing a bottle of champagne.

"Annie and Evey," said Mother.

"Annie and Evey?" I asked, wondering what my sister and Eve Bonham could be planning from 3,000 miles away.

"Yes, isn't it exciting!"

I decided the radio reception wasn't as good as I had thought, or else I had missed a sentence somewhere. But before I could ask Mother to fill in the gaps Father was on the line talking about low pressure over the Azores, and it was time to give the radio a rest. I told Mother and Father I would try to call them through Boston as I neared the New England coast, although they weren't to bank on it. Then I put in

another order for a hot bath, meal, and bed just in case they hadn't got the message, and signed off.

While still tuned into Halifax Radio I heard their weather forecast. It was gloomy to say the least. The BBC had given southwesterly Force 5, but that had been optimistic by a degree of five. The wind was nothing more than a breath, and the Canadian forecast confirmed it. Wind variable and likely to remain so, they said. I put my ETA back to some time in late September and settled down to sit through what promised to be a long calm.

In gales you can at least do something to make yourself go backward, sideways, or even forward. But in calms there is very little to be done. With a stretch of the imagination you can believe you are moving very slightly. But as soon as you chuck an empty packet of Coco Crisps over the side you realize you have the choice of circling the packet clockwise or anticlockwise and in a short time you swear you'll never eat Coco Crisps again.

I had plenty of distractions from my vain attempts to point the *Golly* west. First a seal popped his head up beside the boat. He had angelic eyes with long lashes and the most soulful expression I have ever seen. He gave me a long look, pointed his nose in the air, and then slid gently beneath the water. Next to come along and investigate were my friends, the pilot whales. They couldn't follow me because I wasn't going anywhere, but they nosed around all the same, as ponderous and slow as ever. Instinctively I looked for dolphins and sure enough they turned up an hour later. This time there were hundreds of them and the water was covered in diving shapes as far as the foggy horizon. One dolphin gave me a surprise by leaping six feet into the air only two yards away, but generally the creatures weren't interested in me. It was no fun playing with a motionless boat.

After the dolphins had gone, the sea seemed very quiet and I settled down to read a book in the heavy silence. Suddenly there was a sound of breaking water and escaping compressed air. I spun around and saw an enormous black shape surfacing alongside. It was very large and very black and it was a whale. This one made the pilot whales look like midgets. It was at least as long as the *Golly*, but probably nearer 50 feet. I couldn't be sure because I couldn't see either his nose or his fluke, just his back. The hiss of compressed air went on and on as the great creature blew. Then, neatly closing his blow hole, he slid beneath the surface leaving nothing but a few ripples. After a minute or so he broke the surface again some yards ahead, then dived and was gone. Kicking myself for not having grabbed a camera, I tried to identify the creature from my reference book. But many whales were large and black and I could not be certain which type I'd seen. Whatever the species, it was cheering to have seen a large whale, when the Japanese and the Russians were almost fishing them to extinction.

The calm offered an excellent opportunity to get the day's work done quickly. Then I lay about and did nothing except dream of Newport. I couldn't help wondering how it would feel to be among people again. In only four days, or 20 if we were becalmed much longer, I would be a social being again. The first thing I would have to do would be to mend my table manners. Even I had to admit they had become appalling. When I was cooking my eternal cheese, eggs, and tomatoes on toast I would eye the food like a vulture, then grab it and stuff it in my mouth, leaving debris around my chin and over my hands. Any food that I didn't force into my mouth fell on my oilskins or a paper plate if I had remembered one. When eating spaghetti, I held the bowl two inches under my chin and shoveled with a spoon, making loud slurping noises. Strands that weren't shoveled in were sucked in, whipping around the end of my nose. When the main dish was finished I tidied up by licking as much as I could from around my mouth, then wiping the rest with my hand or sleeve. Eating this fast, I usually had to finish off with a loud burp, after which I felt marvelous. But I could see that all this wouldn't do in American society and I would have to make an effort to mend my antisocial habits.

I wondered how the rest of my behavior would stand up to examination. I felt perfectly normal, but that meant nothing. Of course I was in the habit of groaning loudly and rolling my eyes in their sockets, but that usually resulted from a *contretemps* with a cleat. Similarly, any hopping up and down on one leg accompanied by loud mutterings always followed an attack by the companionway sill, which must have been sharpened on a whetting stone. Neither was I talking to myself, apart from the odd remark aimed at no one in particular. These remarks were of the genre, "well done" as I lost another sail tie over the side, or "brilliant" as I made the wrong sail change yet again. Sometimes I became quite verbose and remarked, "Marvelous! At this rate you'll be there by Christmas."

On the whole I disliked the sound of my own voice and certainly never thought out loud. Talking to someone on the radio was different of course. And filming should have been too. Yet I couldn't believe I was really speaking to living people when I faced that camera, so it was just the same as if I were talking to myself. In time I began to resent this and focused my discontent on the lens that stared at me so coldly from the camera on the stern. One day it finally became too much for me. Turning on all the equipment, I started making my usual type of report about the weather and the progress I was making. Then, in the middle of a long rambling talk about the fascination of whales, I suddenly grunted. I followed this with a growl and a pronounced squint of the eyes. Carrying on normally, I then opened my eyes into a wide stare and gnashed my teeth. The lens stared back at me, completely unimpressed. But by this time I was beginning to enjoy myself.

"I'm feeling well," I continued, thrusting my chin forward and giving a series of monkeylike grunts. "If a little strange," at which I gave my best impersonation of an orangutan with plenty of armpit-scratching and knuckle-trailing. Grabbing a banana from the galley I ate it with my back to the camera, throwing sly and threatening looks over my shoulder. and, just to leave the BBC in no doubt, I finished with a fine impersonation of a gorilla rushing at a camera, with lots of chest-beating and loud shrieks.

The thought of the BBC viewing the reel made me giggle with delight. What on earth would they think of it? And the more I imagined the scene the more I grinned with anticipation. I could see the studio, the technicians, everyone watching, all thinking I had finally eaten too many bananas. Then a less pleasant thought occurred to me. Supposing they used it in the finished film? No, no of course they wouldn't . . . . or would they? If they did, everyone would think I was mad. Did I mind them thinking that? Yes. And with that I threw the reel over the side. But it had served its purpose. I rather enjoyed filming for the last few days of the voyage.

I decided that three and a half weeks alone at sea had also made me self-indulgent. I slept when I wished, read, and ate when I wished. Indeed where else could one sleep between courses, or read a whole book at one sitting? But while reading was socially acceptable, sleeping between courses was not, unless one had an understanding hostess who could clear the table without disturbing one's head.

After seven hours there was still not a breath of wind and I listened anxiously for the next weather forecast from Halifax. But it was no better. Indefinite calm was predicted for the Nova Scotia coast. There was a stationary high-pressure system over the whole area. Yet there was a small ray of hope for me. A low-pressure system had come in over New England. That too threatened to become stationary, but if I could get to the edge of it, I should find wind there.

But the sea remained like a mill pond. Now and then I would imagine a breath of wind on my cheek, but then it would be gone. After 12 hours I had almost given up hope. It seemed as though we would be trapped forever in that foggy windless sea. Then, unbelievably, I felt a breath of wind. It died, but then another came. For two hours these tantalizing breaths came and went until, at last, a gentle breeze came up from behind. I rushed to put up the spinnaker, whereupon the wind veered to the opposite direction and I had to take it down again. Back it went aft, up went the spinnaker, around went the wind again, down came the spinnaker. By this time the foredeck was a mess of tangled ropes and booms and spinnakers and, by the time I had sorted it all out, it was three in the morning. Yet it was good to be moving again and I did not begrudge the sleepless night spent nursing the boat through endless wind shifts.

By morning I was deeply tired and longed to sleep. At seven I was due to call Jack Hill in Lymington and could only snatch half an hour before it was time to switch on the engine and warm up the transmitter. I had arranged to call Jack at 1100 GMT throughout the race but, as I traveled west, this hour became earlier and earlier by local time. Now, as I approached the American coast, I made my call to Jack before breakfast, never one of my brightest moments even when well rested.

That morning I settled down to listen for Portishead, but there was a great deal of static and interference. I gathered from the conversations in progress that there was worldwide radio interference from electrical storms and unusual weather systems. I could see that it was going to be a difficult and lengthy radio session. But I had to try to get through otherwise people would worry. Jacques was due to fly to America the next day, Friday, July 2, and I wanted to send him a message saying that it would be far too difficult to phone him before he left and that he wasn't to expect a call. But how to get through to Lymington? I waited a long time for a suitable gap between conversations, and then yelled down the mouthpiece. I was immediately drowned out by large ships, so I tried another frequency. This time I found one that was free and inviting calls. I yelled again, but there was nothing. They just couldn't hear me. I kept trying and trying as the minutes ticked away. At last one operator picked up my signal, just managed to get my position, but then lost me. Although I continued to try, I never got through again.

It was the first time I had failed to make contact and, in my overwhelming tiredness, I found it very worrying and depressing. The trouble was I had got through so well before — on time and without too many difficulties — that everyone had started to take my calls for granted. I was worried sick in case they should now think something terrible had happened.

I kept calling for another hour, then decided to try through Ocean Gate, the U. S. long-distance station. This was a sobering experience. I realized how spoiled I had become after using Portishead so long. Ocean Gate answered me all right, but then put me on to somebody called a "marine operator," a lady with the broadest accent I have ever heard. The first sign of trouble came when another operator started talking over us on the same frequency. When this was cleared up, my marine operator then told me I could not call England "collect" and seemed unenthusiastic when she discovered I had no account with them. Another operator came in over us, and at that point I gave up.

Why I didn't try Halifax in the first place I don't know, but I thought I would be out of range. But not at all, I got through to the Canadians straightaway and how efficient and courteous they were. There was no problem about reversing the charges, and as I waited for the call to be connected, I could feel the beginning of relief.

When they came back to me, I was stunned. The call had been refused. I couldn't believe it, surely there was a mistake. But no, the call was refused; Mr. Hill was out and would I call back in four hours.

After three solid hours at the radio, after all the effort and disappointments, after so long without sleep, this completely crushed me. All I had wanted to do was leave a message. Just to talk to one of Jack's family for a moment and ask them to speak to Jacques for me. My morale was never lower than at that moment. In four hours I would probably be out of range of Halifax, which could be worked from only 300 miles away, so I would be well and truly cut off. It was a lonely feeling.

I was so tired and upset that I couldn't sleep. And for once I was uneasy. I should be happy that the wind had held, but I was only aware of the oppressive fog that never went away. I wrote in my log "A bad day," and that summed it up. I tried Halifax four hours later but, as I had feared, they could not hear me. Neither could any other station, it seemed. It should not have mattered, not being able to get through, because Jack would know I was all right from the Halifax call. Buy my spirits were at such a low ebb, the tiredness so overwhelming that I could only feel a despair quite out of proportion to the situation. It was a physical thing I am sure. I had been tired for three and half weeks and it took only one night's lost sleep to set me back into exhaustion and tears.

The strange atmospherics also upset the receipt of radio signals from the radio beacons and I could not trust them for my navigation. I managed to pick up Cape Cod beacon when halfway across the gap between Nova Scotia and Massachusetts, but I never seemed to make much sense out of its signals and I spent much of the next night trying to fix my position from inadequate data. The soundings never matched the position I obtained from bearings, and when I should have been crossing the northern end of the George's Bank, the echo sounder told me I was still in deep water.

Finally, I managed to get a little sleep and, with those few hours of rest, I felt refreshed and renewed. I tried Ocean Gate again and persevered with them until I got through to Jack Hill. Ironically, Portishead had phoned him up and given him my position so, no longer worried about me, he had gone out never thinking I would bother to call again. And I needn't have worried about Jacques either. Thinking I might arrive before the Fourth of July, he had caught an early flight to Boston and left a message that I shouldn't bother to call him that night.

So all my worrying and long hours at the radio had been unnecessary. And yet they had seemed so vital at the time. I realized I should have forced myself to sleep instead of wasting so many hours. But the need to talk to someone had been very strong and I reflected that the voyage would end none too soon, either for me or my sense of humor, which was wearing a bit thin. I never actually roared with laughter when I tripped over a stray rope, but I could usually appreciate that it might look funny to a casual onlooker, were there one about. The previous day had been black, but now, on Friday the second, just two days before I hoped to arrive, I was determined to finish happily, in good spirits, still laughing, if it killed me.

So volatile are one's feelings when tired, and so susceptible to atmosphere, that just by willing it, I cheered up immensely. To improve matters a hot sun appeared above and, although it didn't burn all the fog away, it brightened the sea and sky until they were a warm and friendly blue.

I began to appreciate how near I was to land and the finish too, and felt the first stirrings of excitement. Just a day or two away and the burden of worry and anxiety would be gone. It was only as the burden began to lift that I realized how heavy it had been. I only now began to understand that, within two short days, I would never have to go through any more of those long sleepless nights again. The dream, the beautiful dream, of that capable warm voice saying, "Sleep, it's my watch now" would be a reality. At the same time I felt the beginnings of a tremendous satisfaction. I was almost glad that I had been through so much now it was nearly over.

I had one trying moment that Friday that caused my fragile sense of humor to disappear. We were just to the north of the George's Bank and there was a large swell running off the shallows. Despite the light wind, this swell became steeper and steeper, probably as a result of a sharp rise in the seabed. From the size of the waves one would think it was blowing a stiff breeze. But the wind was light and, without the power to drive her through the seas, the *Golly* stopped dead. I tried everything I knew to persuade her to move, but she wallowed helplessly. It was even more frustrating than being becalmed because, although there was wind, we could make no use of it. I made a couple of halfhearted attempts to see the light side of the situation, but failed miserably, and was driven to pouring myself a small dram, or it might even have been three.

Just as I was contemplating giving myself a treat in the form of another, very tiny sip, the wind veered and increased and we suddenly tore off toward the Nantucket Shoals. If I had been to the south that wind shift would have been most unkind, but for once it had paid to be too far north. Even better, the fog cleared for a while and I was able to take a sun sight. And, to crown everything, that evening I saw the first sunset I had seen in 26 days.

What a fabulous night followed. There were bright stars in a clear sky. The wind was free and fast, so that the *Golly* sped along, leaving trails of phosphorescence in her wake. The self-steering took this burst of speed with ease, creaking and groaning from time to time, but holding well as the great paddle swung quickly from one side to the other, correcting the course. One can sail for years to find a night such as that — a warm breeze, a steady sea, and harbor just a day away.

I tried to radio Boston to speak to my parents and Jacques in Newport, but the static was as bad as ever, and this time I was not going to spoil my night's rest by continuing to try.

The next day I had to round Nantucket Shoals, and then it would be less than a day's sail to Newport. The outer, southern limit of the shoals was marked by the Nantucket Lightship, but this was not a mark of the course and unless one wanted to waste a hundred miles, one turned across the shoals themselves. The question was, where? At its most shallow, the water over the shoals was theoretically deep enough for a yacht, being in the region of 9 to 12 feet in places. But one only had to look at the chart to see what the shoals promised for a small boat. There were places called Great Rip and Bass Rip, where the water was severely disturbed. And the ominous words "heavy breakers" could be seen at several points. Shallow water was well known for its ability to turn a gently ocean swell into a series of large white-crested breakers that could pick a yacht up and throw her down onto the sea bottom. The thought of this happening to the *Golly* made my blood run cold. Adventure was one thing, but I put this under the heading of madness and, although it was going to cost me a detour of 50 miles to avoid the shallowest water, I thought it well worth it.

By the next morning I had made my detour and was heading into water no shallower than a good ten fathoms. There had been a heavy swell at the edge of the banks, where the water was squeezed up by the rapidly rising seabed, but after that, the swell became gentle again. It was warm and sunny, though foggy at the same time, as it so often was in that area, making a sun sight impossible. But I was fairly confident of my position and, when I estimated it was safe to do so, I turned the *Golly* on to the heading for Newport. This was a milestone indeed, and my excitement was getting to the pitch where I smiled much of the time, anticipating that moment of arrival. I went over every detail in my mind several times — how it would be, how Newport would look, how I would open that bottle of champagne, how it would be the Fourth of July, just as I had hoped. I estimated my time of arrival as 4 A.M. on the Fourth of July, not an ideal time for the welcome I knew that the family, Ron, and Joan were planning, but it couldn't be helped.

As I sat in the cockpit going through that first dinner menu ashore, course by delicious mouth-watering course, I grappled with reality in the form of lunch. I had set my heart on a cheese sandwich, but the mildew had beaten me to it. The last two loaves, although soft and moist, had been completely penetrated by the dreaded mold. I cut more and more away until I had a piece of bread the size of a matchbox in my hand. Full of anticipation, I cut it open, but there too, was a triumphant patch of green. So I had a soggy biscuit instead, followed by the last tomato, and a banana that didn't like sea air. Mold had crept over all the food that had become damp, and that was everything but a few packets of flour and 22 parcels of All Bran. They were just soggy. The tins were a universal rust color and some were letting in air fast, so that the contents went bad and oozed undesirable substances into the bilge. The eggs were still fresh, but so numerous I didn't know how I was going to explain them away to Mother. And there was a nasty smell from somewhere in the back of the galley, which I didn't have the heart to investigate because I had the feeling it might be an opened tin of plums I had mislaid some weeks before. I still had two tins of plums left, which was about right at my present rate of consumption, but I still had another 50 of various other fruits, not to mention a complete range of vegetables that I had not touched. There was enough food left for an army.

At midday the fog cleared. I should take a sight, of course, I thought, but I leaped instead into my tropical kit of shorts and blouse. This was real tanning weather. As I lay there willing the sun to cook me to a nice golden brown in 20 minutes flat, I suddenly pricked up my ears. That was a strange sound. Rather like breaking water. Faster than a rabbit out of a hat, I leaped to my feet and froze. Ahead was a wall of breakers. I think I may have whimpered in the moment before I groped for the self-steering control and put the *Golly* about. And I certainly had to sit down for a long while after. Without doubt I was too old for all this. Thirty was a good age for retirement from this sport, and I probably should have made it 25. I could tolerate the general excitement, but not the sudden surprises. In my present state of mind, all I needed was to find a giant squid in the sailbin.

After deciding that I must have turned for Newport too soon and that the soundings on the chart bore absolutely no relation to the bottom I had passed over, I tacked again, passed around the shoal and headed for Newport once more. There were no more shoals ahead and hopefully, no more surprises. Just the finish, not a moment too soon.

12

As if sensing the land ahead, the *Golly* flew into the gathering darkness at a steady 7½ knots. Sitting watching the last of the bright red and gold sunset a euphoria crept over me. I allowed myself to realize that I was arriving, that in a very short time the damp and discomfort would be over, and it was a matchless feeling. I felt light-headed from the sensation of speed as the *Golly* rushed across the red-tinted water, but also from the knowledge that, one way or another, I had managed to dodge icebergs, freak waves, and ships pouncing out of the fog. I had even managed to keep that self-steering in one piece and I now eyed the cat's cradle of lines that supported it with the pride of a successful creator.

I had hoped to make the crossing in 28 days, but now it would be nearer 29. I had not quite maintained my average of a hundred miles a day, but in view of all that had happened I was very pleased to have come anywhere near it. After losing at least two days along the way, I was still going to arrive in time for the American Bicentennial.

There was only one problem. I had not been able to contact anyone since my lengthy attempts to call Jack Hill and my family would have no idea that I was just 35 miles from the finishing line off Newport. I was longing to let them know because they would be desperate for news. Also, from a purely selfish point of view, I wanted to be met and towed in. I knew that, whatever the hour, they would come out to meet me and it would be a terrible disappointment for all of us if I sailed into harbor unannounced. Moreover, I didn't want to attempt the entry to crowded Newport Harbor alone and under sail. It would be a fine finish to my voyage if I sank a moored boat.

There was still a lot of lightning about, but I finally made crackly contact with the Newport Coast Guard station and asked them to pass my position and ETA to the organizers. For some reason this message never got through, although the Coast Guard and the organizers were meant to be in constant touch. Not that it mattered, for the wind started to die and the *Golly*'s speed dropped to six then five knots, putting my time of arrival further and further back.

I kicked myself for having sent such an optimistic time. It was inevitable that the wind would immediately decrease and probably die away altogether. The local forecast predicted moderate southeasterly winds, veering to southwesterly, then northwesterly "later on Sunday." I had thought, plenty of time to arrive before it veers around on to the nose. Whereupon it started veering and didn't stop swinging around until it was coming from dead ahead, and it wasn't even Sunday. When Sunday did arrive, the wind then completed its masterful counterstroke by dying away to a flat calm.

My first instinct was to send another message giving an ETA of 9 A.M. But I decided to give my position only and let my family guess when I might arrive according to the wind conditions. This time I contacted another coast guard station, at Point Judith. Through the bad static we had trouble establishing the boat's name. The operator ended up by calling her Robertson's Folly, which I thought quite appropriate. Anyway it was a lot better than the British coast station that had signed off, "Don't hesitate to call us if you get in a jam." The American coastguardsman was very helpful and he agreed to phone my family as soon as he had finished speaking to me.

I didn't dare sleep that night, nor did I want to. Instead I played tape after tape of music and sat looking at the flashes of lightning that showed white on the horizon. I had only a vague idea of my position because the static made the reception from radio beacons very poor and I hadn't got much else to go on. But I was used to that and waited patiently for either land or wind to appear, preferably both.

At last a faint breeze came up from the north and by five in the morning I had the pleasant surprise of seeing Gay Head light on Martha's Vineyard flashing to starboard, about two hours earlier than I had expected. At seven o'clock I was still creeping nicely along and reckoned I would arrive by nine or ten. I was anxious to tell my family this news and tried to call the marine operator in New Bedford so that I could be connected into the telephone system. The New Bedford marine operator was the same kind of lady as the one at Ocean Gate, very brusque, very efficient, and utterly terrifying. Not sure of the right procedures, I called tentatively a couple of times but was quite relieved to find that the formidable lady couldn't hear me. But someone else did. The kind and generous U.S. Tobacco Company had set up a special race liaison office, whose radio was manned 24 hours a day. Not only did they reply to my call, but also they knew exactly where to contact my family and how to organize boats for them to come out and meet me.

There was no time to lose. I rushed below and got out a mirror. By showing my best profile and keeping the sun behind I looked more or less presentable, but in any other light it was enough to make anyone weep. I looked shocking. Despite frequent coverings of cold cream, administered in the general direction of my face, my skin was dry and taut. One smile and I had the feeling it would crack and crumble

169

into a thousand pieces. There were at least one and a half new lines under my eyes and there were two great furrows between my brows from screwing up my tired eyes against the light. To make matters worse, I had spots. Disgusted with the standard of the cuisine, I had taken to eating chocolates and dates and other sickly food. Bright red beacons glowed from my forehead, while my neck was covered in a series of angry bumps.

Even if my face was a disaster I could at least be clean and scrubbed. Before the start I had made several supercilious comments about being cleaner than the men who, it was well known, hardly ever washed at sea. But I had to admit that, apart from the three occasions when I had braved the cold and dabbed at myself with a washcloth, I too had joined the realms of the great unwashed. Taking my example from the Elizabethans, I had covered myself with more and more talc and deodorant until I smelled like a florist's shop. But now I would have a proper wash. Then I thought of that lovely hot bath waiting for me and how thoroughly I could bathe myself in it and what a lot of precious time I would waste by washing here at the sink. So I reached for the deodorant and, after a liberal spraying, reeked of "Morning Freshness" once again.

However, the one thing I really had to have was shining hair. So I washed it quickly and dried it in the frail early morning sun. I then tried to untangle it with the small comb I used to hold my hair back from my face. After breaking three of the teeth and pulling out more hair than I cared to lose, I hid this second disaster underneath a scarf.

Well, at least I could wear something sensational. Down in the depths of the quarter berth I found my bag full of land clothes. Astonishingly only three layers of clothing were damp and I was able to find two pairs of decent trousers and three blouses from which to choose. I spent half an hour picking out the best combination and carefully put them on. Then three things happened at once. I saw land, Jacques called me on the radio, and my trousers fell down.

The first sight of land after a sea passage never fails to thrill the heart. And this land, solid and unmistakable, was the best land I had ever seen. I would have gazed at it for hours, but I heard Jacques's voice coming over the VHF radio. Rushing down to answer him, my knees suddenly locked together and, as I hopped into the cabin, I was interested to see my trousers looped loosely around my ankles.

Jacques told me he was already on the way out, and no sooner had we finished speaking than I was talking to my parents who were just leaving Newport Harbor on another boat. I was in such a state by this time that I hardly noticed the wind was dying again. Finally it dawned on me that the *Golly* was hardly moving. It would be a poor arrival if I had to drink all the champagne on my own, waiting to crawl over the finishing line. There was only one hope of making the line before the wind dropped, and that was to put up a spinnaker. Hopping along the deck and holding my trousers up with one hand, I pulled out the "salami" and hoisted it, then ran back to winch in the guy and sheet, forgetting to hold up my trousers, which caused me to bottom first into the cockpit. Tearing the trousers off I finished the job in my paper underpants and then hurried below to the radio to tell Jacques to look out for a spinnaker.

"I've got the big red spinnaker up, darling, and I'm about four miles from the line now . . ."

"Love, I . . . ." tried Jacques.

" . . . and about southeast of it . . . well, sort of. Hang on, I'll just look at the chart . . . "

"Love, I know where you are!" said Jacques.

"You do?" I was really impressed. How on earth did he know?

Then I heard a shout and I looked up and, of course, there he was, sitting on the side of a large motor boat just yards away. We laughed and waved and jumped up and down like a couple of banshees. Then I saw that sitting next to Jacques was, of all people, my sister, Annie.

"What are *you* doing here?" I shrieked in a sisterish sort of way. She told me she'd taken one look at the bills the previous Monday morning and booked a flight out.

Jacques and I waved and smiled and I said he looked terrible and he asked me if I'd been eating at all, and then I remembered my paper underpants and shot below to try on another pair of trousers. This pair seemed to fit my new shape very much better and I climbed up into the cockpit with more confidence, only to find they hung around my behind in a baggy sack. Jacques made funny faces and I changed for the fifth time that day, choosing the skimpiest, tightest shorts I possessed.

The next hour or so passed in a daze, but I did register that Bob Saunders and the BBC team were also on board the motor boat and, spreading my arms out wide, I yelled, "Bob, I'm going to take you apart limb from limb and film every second of it," at which Bob smiled and nodded so that I was left with the disconcerting feeling he hadn't heard. Frank Page of the *Observer* was there too. He shouted across the news that I was overall first woman to finish the race, and had beaten the women's record by three days. The *Golly* was the first British monohull to finish.

Another boat arrived to escort me to the line. On board were Mother, Father, Ron, and, another surprise, my crew from the Round Britain, Eve Bonham. We all waved furiously, Mother and Father were speechless, but Ron shouted, "I knew you could do it! I knew you could win!" and Eve yelled, "You're mad, bloody mad!" and laughed so much she nearly fell off the deck.

I opened the special Bicentennial bottle of Moët et Chandon and, whenever I felt the need, took a sip. The line at Brenton Reef Lightship arrived not a moment too soon. As I crossed it, the wind died completely, the spinnaker collapsed, and the champagne hit me like a hammer. By the time Jacques jumped on board I was grinning like a Cheshire cat.

Some newsmen are strange creatures. Whereas Bob and the BBC kept their distance for a respectable time, one news correspondent and photographer leaped on board only minutes after Jacques, so that we had hardly a moment together in private. A few minutes would have made no difference to them, but in the intrusive manner of the media men, they could not leave us alone. Jacques was very angry and I was just bemused. Our reunion, which we had looked forward to for so long, became a bewildering and upsetting experience that culminated in Jacques, normally the mildest of men, threatening to throw the newsman over the side.

Then my sister, mother and father, and Ron came aboard to be hugged. Another bottle of champagne appeared — all was people and happiness, and chatter and giggles (mainly from me).

As if to make up for lost time I talked like a nervous rabbit, fast and without pause. Then all was a daze as we were towed into Newport Harbor, a jumble of boats and people and noise on this, the Fourth of July. At the marina there were more people kindly waving, old friends at the dockside, more noise, much confusion, and then Mrs. Mary Thomas advancing toward me with a beautiful silver trophy for being first woman home. Chaos followed as the most delightful customs officer in the world, George Monk, waited patiently while I searched high and low for the ship's papers and my passport, both of which I had put in a safe place. And then there were cheers as Bill Muessel, the retired Newport coast guardsman and Harbor Master came forward to give me his customary big kiss. Two hours later I was still talking hard and showing no signs of slowing down, so Jacques led me firmly away to the apartment where we were staying and poured me a hot bath from which I had to be pulled out an hour later, fast asleep. I rallied long enough to consume the most delicious lunch — a fresh cheese salad prepared by my sister. Then, not a moment to soon, I fell into bed and, after holding the mattress down to stop it swaying, slept a long and dreamless sleep into which no off-course alarm intruded.

Of the 125 boats that started the 1976 Transatlantic Singlehanded Race, only 73 were official finishers. Another five finished after the official time had elapsed, 40 retired to various ports around the Atlantic, and five sailors were rescued from sinking boats. For the first time in the history of the race there was loss of life. Two days before I arrived, the boat of a Canadian, Mike Flanagan, was found drifting with no one aboard and her skipper was assumed drowned. Perhaps it was inevitable that someone should be lost after four accident-free races, but this sad event was no less tragic.

Unhappily, as the weeks and months passed, it became clear that another tragic accident had also occurred. It was difficult for us to grasp it but, of all boats, it seemed that *Three Cheers* had been lost. The trimaran had been as sturdy and seaworthy as any boat, and Mike McMullen a fine and experienced seaman. It was hard to believe they had met with an accident from which they had been unable to escape. That it was an accident there can be no doubt. Any suggestion that Mike took some drastic action as a result of Lizzie's death just before the race was instantly discounted by those who knew him; he was too well-balanced and considerate of his family to have done such a thing. Months later some yellow wreckage was seen in a position that indicated that Mike had got as far as Newfoundland before the accident occurred. To my mind, there was no doubt that he must have been leading at that point. The eventual winner, *Tabarly*, had lost two days with self-steering problems, and with such an advantage, *Three Cheers* would have had little problem in drawing ahead.

For Mike, life had to be lived adventurously. People may criticize an event for being dangerous and foolhardy, but to prevent such events taking place is to deny one of the essential requirements of the enterprising human spirit. If the many sports that involve risk were banned, some people would still find adventurous things to do because, for them, life would be unacceptably gray without the satisfaction and excitement of a great challenge. And, as Mike always said, one might get run over by a bus for no good reason at all. For him that would have been a great indignity.

But during that first week of July we still had high hopes that *Three Cheers* would turn up at any moment and Newport buzzed with the usual celebrations and hair-raising stories that follow a long ocean race. Soon after my arrival *Tyfoon* came in, the delightful Gustaf as good-natured and cuddly as ever. "Ha!" he cried when he saw me. "You beat me again!" And he stamped his foot in mock anger while a grin spread across his face from ear to ear.

"But, Gustaf, you've always beaten me before!" I pointed out.

"I have?" he replied innocently. "Ah vell, in dat case I forgive you. Ve haf dat champagne now? And perhaps two?"

Gustaf had also experienced technical problems during the race, but then everyone had to some degree. I saw two boats with broken forestays and several with badly torn sails. *Spaniel* had been almost overwhelmed in the bad weather and my Polish friend had woken up to find water lapping around his bunk. Sadly I never met this splendid Pole, for he had gone to New York before I arrived, and I was never able to apologize for my strange radio conversation in the middle of the Atlantic. Another boat that had taken a lot of water in through her hatches was Richard Clifford's *Shamaal*, which had capsized twice. On one of these occasions Richard had been below in the cabin and suddenly found himself standing on the deck head with the cabin floor above his head. Then, as the boat righted herself, he found himself up to his waist in water. He spent many long hours bailing the boat out, only to have the same thing happen again. Among other pieces of gear, Richard lost his compass and navigated for the remaining 2,000 miles with a tiny boy scout's hand compass. But as a Royal Marine, he rather thrived on that kind of thing and horrified me by recounting what fun he'd had on the Nantucket Shoals. "You mean you actually crossed them?" I asked in amazement.

"Oh yes!" exclaimed Richard. "You can find marvelous surfing waves right along the shore there. Nice big breakers. Very exciting!"

I shuddered and asked other competitors if they had also crossed the shallows. Many had gone around them like me, but some had not and freely admitted to having been terrified. One Frenchman had actually gone aground in the breaking surf off Nantucket Island but nonchalantly shrugged the whole matter off.

"I did not *mean* to go there," he said, "but my friend whom I was trying hard to beat, he radioed me from just ahead to say that on no account was I to go too near the shoals because they were very dangerous. And of course I did not believe him. I thought he was trying to put me off a good shortcut. So I turn across, a little too sharply — and boomp!" Whereupon he shrugged again and calmly lit a cigarette. I was surprised his hand was steady enough to hold the match.

I was pleased to see Dominique Berthier, the girl who had been rescued off Brest. She had flown out to Newport to meet Aline Marchand who was expected to finish at any moment. But no sooner had Dominique arrived than we heard that Aline was heading back to the Azores under jury rig after being dismasted. This was sad news for us girls. But, happy to say, the splendid Ida did arrive safely some days later, and from the noise and hullabaloo, the whole of Italian America seemed to have turned out to greet her.

During the week the family and I were there, we tried to give every new arrival something of a welcome, which usually meant accepting a glass of champagne. As I sat on board one of the Royal Navy boats, glass in hand, I suddenly noticed everyone had stood to attention and was shaking hands with a man wearing an endless number of gold stripes up his sleeve. Someone whispered to me that it was the First Sea Lord who was here attending a conference, and that he was personally welcoming each of the Royal Navy and Royal Marine competitors as he arrived. An equerry then made signals for me to be brought forward and introduced.

"How do you do?" I said politely and then unmistakably, I

hiccupped. Smiling weakly I retreated fast and hid behind a friend.

The next Royal Navy competitor to arrive happened to have a particularly good vintage champagne he had carefully brought across the Atlantic, and before long we were sitting in the cockpit discussing wave heights with great sweeps of the arm. Then, just as we were getting to the point where the whale rushed across the bows, everyone was suddenly standing to attention and a voice was saying, "Miss Francis, isn't it?" Pushing the glass behind my back, I stood up quickly. "Hullo," I said, trying not to hiccup. Thankfully none appeared and I was just about to smile when the boat rocked slightly and, losing my balance, I grabbed for a handhold and stood swaying violently. "Quite so," said the Admiral, and turned away.

After that, I made careful inquiries of Services competitors to ensure they had received their official visit before we started the welcoming party.

Sadly, we did not stay long enough in Newport to see Jock Macleod arrive in *Ron Glas,* but amazing news was soon circulating. Evidentally Jock had found it necessary to go on deck to free a halyard and, what was more, it had been blowing a gale, so that he was forced to put on his oilskins. Although one sympathized with Jock over this twist in his fortune, one felt it was only right he should know what the rest of us had to go through as a matter of course. Peter Crowther arrived shortly after Jock, losing his title as the slowest man across the Atlantic by an enormous factor of forty days. The second slowest man, Martin Wills, also put in a fast performance and, after working out the times, Jacques and I sent him a telegram pointing out that, if he stuck to that rate of improvement, he should win the next race.

The week that we spent together in Newport was all too short. Firstly, I had a lot of eating to do. The seafood in Newport is the best I have ever tasted and since I weighed

177

only 95 pounds on arrival I had plenty of room to accommodate it. My favorite meal was clam chowder, followed by sole and salad and finished with an enormous ice cream. Mother watched over me to make sure I finished every mouthful, and Jacques tickled my ribs from time to time to see if there was any more flesh on them. The menu for breakfast was unchanging. Eggs. As we cleared out the *Golly* we found more and more of them, still as fresh as could be. We also found the source of the suspicious smell. It wasn't the lost plums after all (they just looked awful) it was an entire toasted cheese sandwich that had got behind some pans in a deep locker and attracted a forest of mold. It took days to clear out all the tins and clean and repair the equipment so that the *Golly* would be ready to be sailed back to England by my old friend John Campbell and his crew, but it was finally done. I was a little sad to see my self-steering repairs dismantled and the casting properly welded. I had been rather proud of the cat's cradle of lines.

Once the *Golly* was cleaned up, I was off to the beach to start my suntan and catch up on my sleep. Only then, as I lay on the warm sand dozing quietly, did I feel the race was really over.

Would I do it again? Absolutely and unequivocally not. Once had been quite enough and once was probably too often. Yet, even as I thought it, I knew I wouldn't have missed doing the race for the world. I had made it and in a reasonably good time, which, like most of the British entrants was all I had ever wanted to do. I could now enjoy the rich glow of achievement. As this achievement was glowing I noticed with interest that my memory started to ignore those recollections it didn't care to remember. The sheer misery of most of the voyage, the dripping damp, the terrible noise of the gales, the eternal fog, and the itching of a scalp covered in spikes. But I wasn't going to fall at that old hurdle, and forcing my mind to remember every last detail, I was able to say ''Never again'' with some feeling. It had been an experience that I would look back on with satisfaction when I was

90. But only then, when I was too old to do anything about it, would I allow myself to forget the unpleasant times and think about doing it again.

In the meantime I would sit in a "rose-covered cottage" thinking of other ways to fill my time. But even as I sat in my rocking chair there would be one thing still bothering me. How, despite the many thorough searches of every locker and cubbyhole, could that hairbrush have completely disappeared?

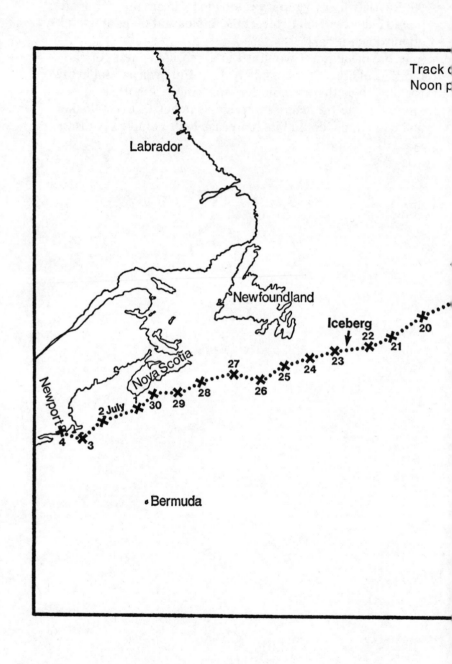

Track o...
Noon p...

Labrador

Newfoundland

Iceberg

22

21

20

23

24

27

25

26

28

29

30

2 July

Nova Scotia

Newport

4

3

• Bermuda

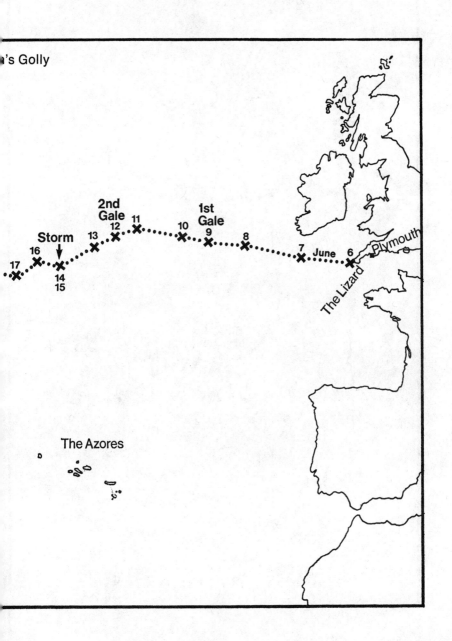

's Golly

2nd
Gale

Storm

1st
Gale

17 16 13 12 11 10 9 8 7 June 6

14
15

The Lizard

Plymouth

The Azores

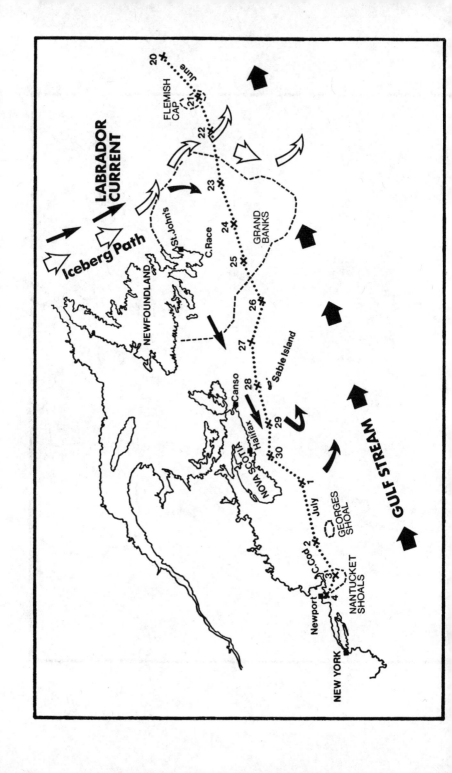

Appendix

General Provisions

6 jars Robertson's marmalade
6 jars Robertson's jam
2 jars Robertson's mincemeat
4 large packets All Bran
4 large packets Prewitt's Muesli
4 packets Jordan's Original Crunchy Cereal
2 packets porridge oats
2 lbs. white flour
6 lbs Felin Geri whole meal flour
3 lns. Granary breadmeal flour
10 oz. dried yeast
22 packets savory rice
3 packets spaghetti
4 packets egg noodles
10 cartons Long Life milk
2 large tins dried milk
1 jar coffee
144 tea bags
1 large tin Ovaltine
2 bottles lime juice
2 bottles lemon and lime juice
2 bottles concentrated apple juice
2 packets brown sugar
1 large can vegetable oil
1 bottle wine vinegar
4 cartons Cup-a-Soup
8 packets dried soup
1 bottle tomato sauce

8 small tins tomato purée
1 jar mustard
1 bottle Worcester sauce
6 jars pickled onions
2 jars honey
1 large bag raisins
1 large bag nuts
6 packets Viota crumble mix
2 packets Viota pastry mix
6 sauce mixes (cheese, white, parsley)
6 packets dried prawn curry
4 pizza mixes
2 packets instant mashed potato
2 packets dried peas
3 packets vegetable stock cubes
1 parmesan cheese
1 jar Marmite
1 tin custard powder
4 packets dates
10 packets oatcakes
3 fruit cakes
11 packets sweet biscuits
8 packets savory biscuits
8 bars chocolate
8 pots fish paste
6 tins sardines
6 tins salmon
   herbs
   pepper
   salt

Tinned Provisions

26	grapefruit/orange juice
10	soup
4	Robertson's new potatoes
4	Robertson's carrots
6	sweet corn
5	tomatoes
3	green beans
5	broad beans
3	baked beans
4	mushrooms
2	spinach
2	stuffed peppers
4	artichoke hearts
8	asparagus tips
20	Robertson's peaches
20	Robertson's plums
10	Robertson's fruit pie fillings
10	Robertson's cherries
10	gooseberries
10	pears
10	mandarin oranges
5	prunes
5	blackberries
6	chestnuts (marrons)
8	cream
8	custard

Fresh Provisions

4	pints milk
3	cartons yoghurt
12	loaves bread
1½	lbs. butter
5	cartons vegetable margarine
10	dozen eggs
5	lbs. cheese
5	lbs. potatoes
15	large onions
4	lbs. carrots
1	cabbage
4	trays tomatoes
1	lettuce
2	cucumbers
8	pears
10	grapefruits
15	oranges
4	bunches bananas
20	apples
15	gallons fresh water